Tim Murphey

Language
Hungry!

An Introduction to Language Learning Fun and Self-Esteem

**HELBLING
LANGUAGES**

Language Hungry!
by Tim Murphey

© HELBLING LANGUAGES 2006
www.helblinglanguages.com

ISBN 978-3-902504-78-4

First published 2006
9   8   7   6   5   4   3
2010   2009   2008   2007

Designed by Gabby Design
Cover by Capolinea
Illustrations by Kaori Miura

Printed by Athesia

Contents

Preface

The chapters in this book were originally created with my students in mind, and I have used much feedback from them in the writing process. The ideas and activities originated from my experiments with students in my classes on Alternative Learning Forms, Interaction and Language Acquisition, and Neuro-Linguistic Programming. Typically, I would present the ideas in class; students would try them out and then tell me what they thought. I would write an article based upon their feedback, then I would give them copies of it and get further feedback ... I learn a lot from my students. I believe all teachers can. And you, too, can learn how to work smart when you listen to your students and get them to do their own research into how they learn best. For both teachers and students it helps to get passionate, to become **language hungry!**

Various editions of *Language Hungry* have been field tested by teachers and learners in Switzerland, Finland, China, Thailand, New Zealand, and Japan. Many of the chapters were first published in *Nagoya Avenues*, a popular Japanese magazine. Learners of languages other than English have told me that my ideas have been useful to them as well.

The emphasis in this book is on learning how to **work smart** through turning on your brain in various ways. In other words, you use your brain instead of letting your brain use you. Can you imagine getting into a car and just letting it take you wherever it wants to go? Well, that's how most people let their brains operate. Too many people spend too much time working too hard. Some people may think that's admirable. But when you learn how to work smart and direct your thinking positively, you can become immensely more productive and have a lot of fun at the same time.

To teachers: when I'm reading an interesting book about teaching, I know that I like to absorb the information and think of ideas for myself before reading about how I can use them. I believe that many teachers are very creative and can imagine how they might use the materials as they read, and I want to allow your creativity to blossom. So it's near the end that I have included a list of notes and suggestions for ways of using the book with students – see Teacher's Notes.

This is a little treasury of serious ideas for enjoying learning and helping others to do the same. It is unconstrained by the usual, and refreshingly free of excessive concern for dignity. Presented with the lighthearted authenticity of an explorer ever willing to learn from his own occasional 'wonderful failures' as well as from his successes. Let's welcome it!"
Earl Stevick, author of *Memory Meaning and Method* (second edition)

Introduction: Go For It!

The information in this book can change your life when you choose to use it and improve yourself. You will learn how to enjoy learning even more passionately than you do now. You can be happier when you welcome new opportunities around you and willingly take healthy risks that will challenge and thrill your mind and body. It's up to you, though, to choose to use the information, to experiment with it, to risk finding more joy in learning. For in the end, you are your own best teacher.

Three suggestions to *get the most out of this book*.
When you really want to understand, after you read … **DO IT!** Actions speak louder than words, and they are far better teachers. Use the Smart Fun sections to experiment with the ideas. You can use them to learn any subject, and to improve yourself. Courageous learners DO IT! (Don't just accept every idea. Challenge each one, and adopt only those ideas which fit you. You can offer the others to someone else.)

Secondly, you can **use your peers to learn more intensively**. Social scientists are now seeing that we learn much more from each other than we do alone. We learn most things when we interact with others. Interaction is doing. Again, good learners dare to interact and learn from each other.

Thirdly, when you really want to learn anything, **teach it to others**. Even if you are still learning it yourself. When you explain and show what you are learning to others, you learn it much better. Research shows that usually you remember:
· 10% of what you read
· 26% of what you hear
· 30% of what you see
· 50% of what you see and hear together
· 70% of what you say, and
· 90% of what you say while doing something such as teaching. (Silverman 1987)
Teaching is learning. When you really want to learn well, teach others. As a teacher, the more often you teach this information to your students, the better you will learn it. The more often students teach these things to each other, the better they will learn them.

Silverman, L. (1987). "Global Learners: Our Forgotten Gifted Children." Paper presented at the Seventh World Conference on Gifted and Talented Children, Salt Lake City, Utah.

DO, Interact, Teach = DO IT !

Thanks to

Thanks to
Kaori Miura for her precious drawings; Ed Skrzypczak, Linda Woo, Rohini Deblaise, Koko Kato, Kaori Murakami, and Millie Grenough for their precise reading and editing; the editors and readers of *Avenues*; Brad Deacon, Lois Conley, Minae Goto, and Yuki Mizuta, for many valuable suggestions and lots of encouragement; my students, graduate & undergraduate, colleagues & friends who have tried the activities and shared their experiences with me. They are still teaching me much. The staff at Macmillan Language House who first published this book in Japan were very helpful. Lucia Astuti of Helbling, the present publisher, was very encouraging and positive about this project and made the editing easy and fun. Caroline Petherick did a wonderful job copy-editing to increase the clarity. The staff and administration of Nanzan University (Japan), Yuan Ze University (Taiwan), Dokkyo University (Japan), and Hawaii Pacific University have shown great tolerance and interest in topics only beginning to be taught on most campuses.

I would also like to acknowledge generous research grants from Nanzan University (Pache I-A) in 1991, 1995, 1996, and 1997 that supported research that had a direct impact on understanding and implementing many of the strategies advocated in this book. Mostly I would like to thank the numerous teachers and students who have shared their excitement over the book with me. I look forward to hearing more from you!

Finally, I would like to dedicate this book to my dear Aunt Patty, Patricia Murphey, who has traveled the world, treasured the variety she found, given laughter and joy from her heart, and inspired all those she came in touch with to do the same – and she is still doing it! With love! mits

> ## DO, Interact, Teach = DO IT !

CHAPTER 1
The Roller Coaster of Your Language Learning

CHAPTER 1
The Roller Coaster of Your Language Learning

"You can't stop the waves, but you can learn to surf."
J Kabat Zinn

Think about it first!
1. When do you feel as though you're improving and doing well?
2. When do you feel as though you're forgetting and not doing so well?
3. How can you control your emotions more?
4. How can you have more good days to enjoy, and relax during the not-so-good days?

Do you sometimes feel as though your language learning has slowed down, or stopped? Or even begun to nosedive dangerously? Have you forgotten what you thought you knew? Nearly all language learners have these feelings at some time. Language learning has ups and downs, and understanding why allows us to relax a bit and find ways to change the direction of the roller coaster when it's going down.

It is a popular idea that when we strive to learn we make steady progress through time. A diagram of it would look something like this:

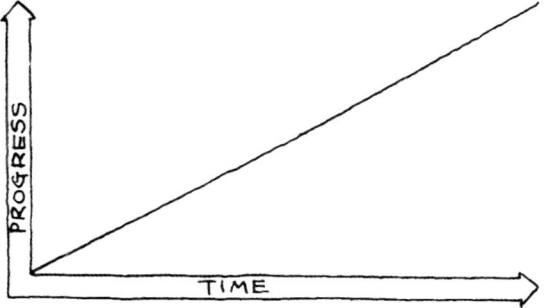

But making such steady progress is rare. More often, progress takes a much more exciting, and at times frustrating, course.

Graphically, it would resemble an irregular roller coaster that nevertheless probably follows the ascending line of our first diagram. If we superimposed the two, it would look something like this:

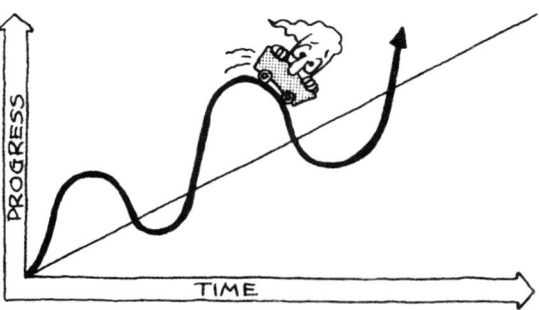

Depending on you and your context, through time the roller coaster will have its own particular shape.

Take a moment and think in which direction your roller coaster is going at the moment. One thing is sure - there will be moments when you feel as though you're going up (progressing) and others when you're going down (regressing). Even if the curve flattens out into a plateau you may have the impression of going down, because of the contrast with the recent thrill of going up. Let me describe what I think happens. You can see for yourself if it fits your experience.

First of all, roller coasting is natural in our learning; we all have progression, levelling out, and going backwards. We have all experienced the euphoria of realizing we've made a leap in learning, as well as the frustration of having forgotten, even if momentarily, what we thought we knew. *Going down, forgetting, is part of the natural swing of progression. We all seem to have, and perhaps need, downtime. What is crucial is sustaining the motivation and interest while we're in the slumps.* Let's also understand that there are several roller coasters rolling at once. In the space of just an hour, learners may have several cycles of feeling: "I can! – I can't! – I'm good at this! – I'm stupid!" These cycles can be more long-term as well; they can last for weeks, months, or years.

There are several reasons why our learning may seem to go up and down, momentarily or for a longer time. Here are a few:

Lack of understanding: When one understands only a little of the language being used, then frustration may set in and our impression of progress seems to backslide. In a classroom, if teachers don't make the effort to find out what their students know, they risk giving input that is too high (and frustrating students) or too low (and insulting them). It feels good to be with people who know how to adjust to your level and talk about things you know how to talk about. But if you don't understand, let your partners and teachers know this. Then they can adjust to you.

Negative emotions: When we don't like the subject, the teacher, or the physical environment, or if we feel a threat to our security (for example, that we'll make a fool of ourselves), we are not very open to learning. In this situation, even if we can understand the input, we spend most of our energy defending ourselves instead of being open to learning. So instead, it's better if we can find people who make us feel good when we speak, and situations that allow us to make mistakes and yet still succeed in communicating.

We can pause and compliment ourselves, too. Give yourself a pat on the back when you realize you've really learned or communicated well. Too often after succeeding, we just turn the page to something new, and continue until we are burnt out. But it's good to pause, instead, to reflect on what we've accomplished; it reinforces our confidence and helps us work more effectively in the long run.

Fatigue: If we're too tired to listen to new information, even if it's easy, enjoyable, and non-threatening, the information just won't go in. When we don't get enough sleep, especially if it's because we've been studying late at night, we may not be alert in class. It's a good idea to get enough sleep and rest when we can. We can also take frequent short breaks, and that way learn much more comfortably.

Information overload and not enough time for recycling: Even when we find the information understandable and we are motivated and rested, our minds still have a limit to the amount of new information that they can easily process. To try and absorb too much new information becomes frustrating in the long run.

New language also needs recycling – using it many times in many contexts – in order for it to stick in our minds. Small amounts of new language met in a short time need recycling in many contexts. Personal use also contributes to how much new language we can process at a time. When we use language for ourselves in everyday conversation, we learn it more quickly. And learning vocabulary doesn't happen all at once. Instead, each time we see, hear or use a word, we know it a little better. It is a deepening process in which we learn vocabulary and grammar through meeting the items many times in many different ways. So it's natural that some words are recognizable but not yet ready to be used. One way to recycle learning is to tell everybody the same thing. For example, on a Monday I can get someone to help me describe my weekend trip in Japanese. Then I can tell many other people the same story for the rest of the week. It's short, it's personal (I did it!), and it's capable of being recycled with many partners.

Competition for attention: If there is an important sporting event that day, or if you are suddenly in love, or if … (any number of reasons) then your attention may go in other directions. If your teacher is clever enough, she or he can use this topic as the subject to talk about that day. Alas, these things are not always written on the foreheads of learners – but you can tell your teacher about them!

Ideally, the above blocks would never exist: learners would always be well rested, get just the right amount of understandable information, and feel motivated and secure, with nothing else to compete for their attention.

But in fact these blocks are common enough to send us roller coasting quite often. However, *just knowing that ups and downs are natural helps you to keep calm when you seem to be going down*; it helps you to look for ways to change the situation; and it helps you to keep your confidence. It is also comforting to know that what goes down can also go up. It depends on how you organize your learning.

Smart Fun!
The Roller Coaster of Progress
1. Where are you now on your own roller coaster of language learning? How often does it change?
2. What things can make it go down and up? List a few.
3. List the things that you can do to make you feel good about your learning. When is the next time you can do each of these things?
4. What things can you do to help a partner?
5. Tell somebody (or several somebodies) about your answers.

If you want to help a language learner, here's what you can do:

1. **Let your partner know that trying is succeeding.** This attitude is especially important at those times when the roller coaster plunges frightfully and they think of jumping out. But you as a helper can make the roller coaster become a fun and relaxing ride.

2. When you see your partner having trouble, **use easier language and topics** that you are sure they know well.

3. **Show that you understand.** Showing that a message has been received makes speakers want to try more.

4. **Use reformulation** instead of correction. Reformulation means repeating what your partners say in a slightly more correct way. A lot of recent research shows that corrections by themselves really don't help learners much (parents don't correct their children when they learn their first language – and yet they learn it). A correction is too often like a cold slap in the face. It's hard on our confidence and it hurts more than it helps. But reformulation, saying it again in your own words, confirms that you understand, and so is encouraging.

5. **Compliment progress.** It makes us want to do more!

CHAPTER 2

Need an ideal conversation partner?
Try a Non-native!

CHAPTER 2
Need an Ideal Conversation Partner? Try a Non-native!

"The invariable mark of wisdom is to see the miraculous in the common."
Ralf Waldo Emerson

Think about it first!
1. How much do you think you can learn from your classmates when you speak to them in the target language?
2. How can you find classmates who want to speak with you outside of class in the target language?

Some researchers are now saying that native speakers are not necessarily the best partners for language learners to talk with. Really! **The best partners for you may be other learners who are at your approximate level, non-native speakers (NNSs) like yourself. Your classmates, for example.**

Of course, this still means that native speakers (NSs) are good partners too. (When you can find them!) They are good models, and interesting. But interaction with NSs is far from ideal.

Why Native Speakers are not always the best partners

1. NSs tend to dominate speaking time, leaving little time for NNSs to take part, even if they want to.
2. There is little *negotiation* of what is said. That means that when NNSs don't understand, they don't ask what things mean. Research shows that much is learned when you ask questions and reformulate to make language understandable. But often, when NNSs don't understand a native speaker, they just accept their confusion silently, with little questioning. Daring to say that you don't understand takes courage. But with other NNSs you dare much more to ask questions and to negotiate meaning.
3. Interaction is usually an exchange of information. The different abilities make most NSs unwilling to talk with NNSs for very long, unless there is some more information to be exchanged.
4. It may not be easy to adjust to a learner's level, even if a NS wants to. It takes an extremely perceptive NS to do quality-adjusting for long periods, and to give the amount of repetition that allows beginners to absorb new language.
5. Often, there simply aren't enough NSs to go around. If you think you can practise only with NSs, then you will be simply out of luck. However, if you consider practising with NNSs, you may find that in many ways they are better than NSs. And they are everywhere!

The Advantages of NNS-NNS Interaction
When you speak with someone who is at about your level, you exchange more

information and language. You still have different vocabulary and different ways to use the language, and you can learn a lot from each other. Within any class, any two students probably have about 70% of their words in common. That leaves 30% that you can learn from each other when you interact. Because you share a lot of the same vocabulary, you understand each other more easily. You are also more relaxed, and less afraid of making mistakes. You are ready to take risks and negotiate, and even to correct each other. All of this means you can recycle new vocabulary and practise a lot.

Also, when you are talking to others who speak your language, you can use it when you really don't understand. And when you share the same culture, it's easier to guess the meaning. Usually with a NS you share neither the language nor the culture, and that can make understanding more difficult.

Does NNS–NNS interaction work?

It works for some people wonderfully, but not for all. Why? I gave the above information to over 80 students at Nanzan University in 1991, and I asked them to experiment with speaking only English with their classmates, in and out of class. The experiment failed wonderfully! Student feedback revealed why it didn't work, and pointed to things that you can do to make it succeed. (You can learn a lot when things don't work and you keep your eyes open at the same time.)

Some students reported that talking in the target language to other non-natives was unnatural and embarrassing, and that there wasn't much time to do it. The experiment was also difficult to carry out because some friends simply refused to talk in the target language. Many commented that speaking their native language is faster and easier. Quite a few felt embarrassed when people looked at them. Some students also expressed the problem of not seeing anyone from the class often enough to practise.

Making it work

Looking more closely at the students for whom it does work shows that they see NNS-NNS interaction as a game, have supportive friends, have special times and places in which to speak, and actually enjoy it when others see them speaking English.

In order to make NNS-NNS talk successful, most of these learners do the following:

1. **Think it's a game, have fun with it!** It's a **fun game** that you can play with certain friends. Think of it as your group's special way to communicate.

2. **Find a supportive friend or two.** Some people will warm to the idea and enjoy the game (which soon becomes reality). Choose partners who are at your approximate level and who have similar interests.

To find partners, send out "feelers" with greetings in the target language ('Good morning!' 'Ohayo!' 'Bonjour!'). Potential partners reveal themselves by responding in the target language, and continuing to talk in it.

3. **A time and place for all things.** Trying to speak the target language ALWAYS may be difficult. Pick certain places and times when you agree to speak (probably not when you are in a large group in which your own language will be spoken). Play the game as long as it is comfortable.

Then take a break when you need to relax. Make the game periods regular, and short. Then increase them when you feel you want more fun. Lunches, coffee breaks, or meetings for activities like bowling seem to work best.

4. You are a target-language speaker. Rather than thinking of yourself as a strange person speaking strangely in public and being stared at, think of yourself as a fascinating person who can speak more than one language. Think that you enjoy being looked at and making people wonder where you come from.

5. Mixed language daijobu. Throwing in a few words of the target language can really spice up your conversation and sometimes get you to switch for a few sentences. 'Honto, it's tanoshii.' 'C'est lustig!' 'Andiamo!' 'Vamos!'

Language clubs work well because they encourage the above ideas.

An analogy with the above tips would be playing tennis. It's a game I love, and I'm fascinated by it. I pick my partners carefully because I know that if they are at about my level I will be challenged, not frustrated (as with professionals) nor bored (as with beginners). If they like tennis as much as I do, we can play often. And of course, there is a time and place for playing tennis, and I take breaks when I get tired. But I also find myself playing the game in my head at strange times and talking tennis with other friends. Instead of being embarrassed when I walk to the tennis courts with my racquets, I think that when people see me maybe they will think about getting some exercise and becoming healthier.

We need sports to stay healthy. We also need to speak other languages to have other points of view and to appreciate the wonderful variety around us. There are many ways to improve our ability to speak. An efficient learner learns not only to take advantage of opportunities but also to **make the opportunities.** There are a lot of people with whom we can improve our speaking ability and have fun at the same time. It just takes changing a few old myths and taking good risks. Then the game becomes reality ... and fun.

Smart Fun!
Try a Non-native

1. Greet (Good morning! Güten Tag! Bonjour! Ohayo! Buon giorno!) at least three of your classmates outside class in your target language every day. Notice which ones respond to you and try to carry on the conversation. Those are the ones you want to pick for your partners.

2. Find a friend in your class, and agree to speak only your target language most of the time for at least four days, in and out of class. How did it go? (It's okay to mix in a little of your native language when the going gets tough, if that's useful.)

3. Find another friend and agree to telephone each other every night for a week and ask each other 1) 'What did you do today?' and 2) 'What will you do tomorrow?' During the day you can prepare the things you're going to say that evening. Ask your partner for the times of day it would be good to call.

4. Talk to a friend about the advantages and disadvantages of speaking with a NS and a NNS.

CHAPTER 3
Appreshiating Misteakes

CHAPTER 3
Appreshiating Misteakes

"You grow up the day you have your first real laugh – at yourself."

Ethel Barrymore (1879—1959) American actress

Think about it first!
1. How do you feel when you make a mistake?
2. How could you feel interestec in your mistakes and even fascinated by them?
3. How can mistakes be helpful?
4. How can mistakes show you that you are learning?

Learners are sometimes stopped not only by their "erroars" but also by their fear of makinc them. When students hesitate to speak for fear of making mistakes, they interact less with others, and thus have fewer opportunities for learning (Beebe 1983, Seliger 1983). Some teachers try to help students by creating a comfortable class and by not correcting very much.

However, *you* can take charge of your own learning much more when you understand how helpful mistakes really are. You can **change the meaning of mistakes**. You could think, for example, "Mistakes are actually wonderful things; they can even help the learning process."

Notice how successful business leaders view mistakes:

You've got to have an atmosphere where people can make mistakes. If we're not making mistakes, we're not going anywhere. Gordon Forward, President, Chaparral Steel

Many people dream of success. To me success can only be achieved through repeated failure and introspection. Soichiro Honda, founder, Honda Motor Company

[Les Wexner, founder of Limited Inc] *actually likes mistakes; buyers are graded not only on their successes, but also on their failures. Too many hits means the buyer isn't taking enough chances.* Forbes, April 1987.

How can you learn to like mistakes?

It's important to learn to laugh at your mistakes. Tell stories, in a humorous way, of yourself making mistakes. For example: *One day when I leaned on my umbrella going up an escalator in a large store, it got stuck in the grooves. I had to hit the emergency button to stop the escalator. All the people had to walk by me as I excused myself. But they all smiled and laughed a bit at me as they passed by and said, "No problem." I was sooo embarrassed! Then I realized that I had made a lot of people happy by changing their routine day, and that was nice.*

When I tell this story in my mistakefully joyous Japanese to my Japanese students, I'm using mistakes to tell a story about a mistake and allowing them to see that it still succeeds. It does this in two ways – I can make people happy, and I can communicate despite making mistakes. I'm modelling what I want them to do in English. The ideas that follow will help change mistakes into fascinating wonders that become useful instead of painful.

JUST DO IT!

Task 1: Think of a small mistake that you made recently, and tell as many people as you can about it in a humorous way in your target language. Use short sentences and mentions (see Mentions at the end of this chapter, page 23). This is a lot of fun and naturally 'changes history' as you do it. Problems are tamed by our laughter.

Task 2: Make a small mistake on purpose. When you do it, notice the reactions of the people around you. Notice that other people usually either don't notice or don't care. You may even want to build mistakes into your natural charm, as Tomomi did:

*I put [salad] dressing on rice! A friend of mine found it immediately and said, "What are you doing? It's dressing!" I told them that I had done it on purpose. But they didn't believe me so I told them the reason [homework]. Then they understood. I think making a mistake on purpose is sometimes useful because we had a dinner in a congenial atmosphere. In addition, **if I make such a mistake again, they may think that I did it on purpose!!** I'm going to make a mistake again because it's funny!* (Tomomi Sugiyama, my emphasis)

Knowing you are making a mistake, and observing feedback from those around you, allows you to naturally separate yourself from the mistake itself. If you can do this often enough, unplanned mistakes which happen will also spark the same reaction. Simply feeling terrible about making a mistake usually stops us from learning. But when you can look more objectively at what happens, you can decide if there is any good information there for you to learn from. Or you can decide to ignore it or laugh at it. You can put your emotions on hold instead of letting them put a hold on you. The next two tasks are ways you can interrupt patterns and break an automatic negative reaction to mistakes.

Task 3: Visualising positive reactions

You can do this in your head right now.

Imagine a little mistake that you will probably make in the next 24 hours, perhaps a recurring small mistake like forgetting something or tripping. Got one? Now, see yourself in your mind making the mistake, and then see yourself **responding as you would like to respond**, in a way that you think would be helpful. For example, laughing and thinking, "That shows how wonderfully human I am; I am consistent, a perfectly imperfect me!" (Pause here until you've done this.) Got it? Great! Now, run a film loop of yourself through your mind, making the mistake with this positive response several times. Notice later what happens when the mistake actually occurs.

Task 4: Dealing with the voice

When I'm playing tennis, I sometimes make stupid shots. I used to have this little voice in my head that would say, "You stupid "#@! *(editor deletion)*" I noticed that once I let that voice get into my head, I usually couldn't play very well for quite a while – the voice was so loud! So I then did two things that you can try on yourself, if you too have one of those voices:

First, I took the key word of my internal voice, "stupid", and tied it to "interesting and funny" in my head. I simply repeated "stupid – interesting and funny" ten times in my head, and it made me smile. Now, when I hear the word "stupid" either in my own head or from someone else, I tend to think, "Hey, there's probably something interesting and funny here," and I can look at things more objectively, less judgmentally. "Stupid", after all, is just a judgment and not much help. It shuts down the mind when it most needs to open up.

Secondly, I listened to the horrible tone of the voice in my head and tried changing it to something more helpful. I shifted it into Mickey Mouse's voice. Now when I hear it I immediately see Mickey Mouse, and I laugh instead of cringing.

And in addition, I realize that the voice really wants to help me, but that it just didn't know how to do it.

Mistakes, then, show that you are taking risks to learn more. If you haven't made many mistakes lately, you can risk a bit more to learn more efficiently. Walking is a process of continually being off-balance and catching yourself. In learning languages especially, daring to stumble, trip, and even crawl will at least get you somewhere. Someone who is too afraid of stumbling gets nowhere. Remember, *a journey of a thousand miles may begin with a small trip.* You might as well enjoy it!

Smart Fun!
Appreshiating Misteakes
1. Make a mistake on purpose and write about it.
2. Michael Jordan said, "I am not afraid of failing, but I will not accept not trying." How much have you been trying? And what more can you try that will help you learn?
3. Try having a mention conversation with a friend every day (see below). Agree to try to keep the number of words to a minimum, and find out as much as you can!
4. What mistakes have you made recently in your target language? How do they show that at least you are trying?

MENTIONS, AND THE MYTH OF COMPLETE SENTENCES

Many of us are under the impression that we speak in complete sentences. Wrong! In fact, linguists estimate that of everyday native speech, more than 50% is just fragments, pieces of sentences; in a rich, shared context, we "mention" only the essential words needed to exchange messages.

Many learners do not speak aloud because they are trying to think of long, complete sentences in their heads. Teachers and friends who are trying to help us to speak "correctly" often give us too many words and ... Bang! Overload! Our short-term memory explodes! We just can't hold it long enough to put it into long-term memory.

But often just a few words would be more efficient. Only later do we start combining all the little pieces, which by then have become automatic, into longer sentences. So if you notice yourself getting frustrated, keep it short. Go for short sentences. All-purpose ones. Keep things simple. Keep 'em short. Go for it! Risk a little! Like this!

Quotes in this chapter taken from:
Peters, Thomas (1989). *Thriving on Chaos* London: Pan books, p. 259.

Beebe, Leslie M. (1983). Risk-taking and the language learner, in *Classroom Oriented Research in Second Language Acquisition*, H.W. Seliger & M. H. Long (editors) Cambridge, Mass. : Newbury House.

Murphey, T. (1994). Mentions in actions, *TESL Reporter* 27, pp. 21-26.

Seliger, Herbert W. (1983). Learner interaction in the classroom and its effects on language acquisition, in *Classroom Oriented Research in Second Language Acquisition*, H.W. Seliger & M. H. Long (editors) Cambridge, Mass. : Newbury House .

* I want to thank Steve Andreas, Charles Adamson, Barbara Waggoner, Rohini Deblaise, and Veli-Matti Toivonen for input concerning this article, and of course my students, for sharing their valuable mistakes with me, especially Yuki Mizuta (the escalator story) and Tomomi Sugiyama.

Remember, a journey of a thousand miles may begin with a small trip.
So you might as well enjoy it!
Tim Murphey

CHAPTER 4
Shadowing, Summarizing, and Self-Talk: Letting Your Mind Do the Talking

CHAPTER 4
Shadowing, Summarizing, and Self-Talk: Letting Your Mind Do the Talking

"Celebrate what you want to see more of."
Tom Peters

"Silence is ... golden.
A pause is worth a thousand words."

Anon

This chapter is about putting a foreign language into your head. It's about shadowing and echoing (mentally repeating) what you hear. And it's about talking to yourself in the target language. These are the ways in which babies and children pick up language – their brains do it naturally. Unfortunately, when we learn a foreign language we sometimes don't remember to do this.

When babies learn speech, they typically babble the last sounds they hear. So when Mum says, with a tickle, "Is baby happy?", the baby joyfully responds with the last syllable, "py py py," and Mum, of course, knows exactly what baby means.

The last sounds in a stream of words are more memorable than the others because you can hear the echo during the pause. Those last sounds have a chance to echo in our brains. So if I spoke this sentence to you now, and I paused after the full stop, the easiest part for you to remember would be the last word because it would echo in your brain (**brain bra**in brain ...). This happens not only for babies, but also for learners of foreign languages.

Part of improvement in language learning is being able to increase the number of words we can repeat. We can exercise our short-term memory muscles by continually trying to repeat longer and longer phrases. When I first came to Japan,

I was hearing things like 'xxxxxx mashou' and 'xxxx desune', so I had 'mashou' and 'desune' ringing in my ears all the time. Finally I asked what a 'mashou' and a 'desune' were, and I found that they must be very funny things, because everyone laughed every time I asked. ('Mashou' means 'let's' and is a grammatical verb ending; 'desune' is like a tag question.)

ECHOING THE LAST PART OF SENTENCES

The point is that our brains naturally want to echo. And we can encourage our brains to do it more. Our language learning may progress faster if we exercise this natural echo. Let me tell you what I've done experimentally, and you can try it out for yourself and see how it works for you.

JUST DO IT!

Task 1: Shadowing
I ask learners to shadow my speech as I talk. For example, / I make a pause / that is as long / as the utterance / wherever / there is a slash. / At first/ I start out repeating my words (I start out repeating my words) / under my breath (under my breath) / just after I have said them (just after I have said them). / Then gradually,

(then gradually) / the echo gets so soft (the echo gets so soft) / that the learners only have the **shadow** (that the learners only have the shadow) / in their brains (in their brains), / not out loud (   )./ It's important / to keep the chunks small / at least at first. / Any instructions / or a story / can be told / in this way./

In the pauses, you have time to repeat the words, and you can think about their meaning. Amazingly enough, when I notice my students shadowing me, I tend to slow down and speak better, and their comprehension and confidence go up. It's lovely!

It's important for teachers, when speaking in short phrases, to vary their intonation and the way they speak. If they don't, it may sound monotonous and put people into a hypnotic trance called sleep! It may seem artificial at first, but it soon gets to be fun, and is really easy to understand. One important thing: keep your pronunciation normal – just make smaller chunks and longer pauses.

Task 2: Echoing

Shadowing is difficult without someone who is willing to speak in small chunks and leave pauses. So when speakers use long phrases, try **echoing** just the last few words that you hear (that you hear). You can also do this with a conversation partner. In pairs, tell each other about your weekends, or something very familiar. While one person speaks, the other tries to echo the last few words of each statement. By repeating the last few words, you can retain the information better and also learn new vocabulary. And doing this has the added advantage of letting the speaker know that you are really listening.

Task 3: Summarizing

My students tell me that it is very helpful after shadowing to *summarize* what you've just heard. Just say, "Let me see if I

have understood. You say you ..." Summarizing immediately after hearing something really increases your ability to remember the language as well as the content.

Shadowing and Summarizing are great ways to interact and learn! And they go together really well.

Task 4: Self-talk

Not too long ago, many people thought that talking to yourself meant you were crazy. People were thought to be witches for admitting that they heard voices in their heads.

In the 1920s, Piaget and Vygotsky studied this naturally occurring egocentric/inner speech, and now some cognitive psychologists are suggesting that unless you do have voices in your head, you are not using your brain very well (Smith 1983). **In fact, intelligent and creative people may do more self-talk than out-loud talk as they explore, revise, and create with the many voices in their own minds.**

Self-talk helps us to get things done as we talk our way through the day. We may talk to ourselves especially in stressful situations, such as while driving a car or striving to win in sports. Self-talk helps us plan important conversations. We also think of things we should have said after conversations, as we relive them.

We all use a lot of self-talk in our native language naturally, but we seldom think of using it in the language we are learning. We may assume that talking to oneself in a foreign language is a sign of an advanced learner. But it could also be a strategy to become advanced.

Waking up in the morning and talking to yourself in your target language is also a great way to get your brain on track before a test. Speaking of simple things can do a lot ("Now, I'm going to take a shower and feel good ..."). After a while, it becomes a habit. Now, when I look for something in my office, I involuntarily utter, "Doko des ka? (Where is it?)"

You can use your target language to describe your routines (what you do every day), and learn quickly and easily. First, learn the language to describe the routine, and then practise it. Because you are talking about things you do regularly, you will recycle the language often.

Task 5: Planning

You can also plan a conversation that you are going to have. It really helps you when you then actually have that conversation. Many people tell me they run a film in their minds of a planned meeting. They hit the pause button when they need time to think of what to say next, then run the film through several times without pauses, and with various alternate scenarios. What happens when they actually have the conversation may be very different – but they say they feel more comfortable and confident because they have a lot of language ready and waiting.

Some people find sleeping on conversations very helpful.

They imagine a conversation that they are going to have the next day, and plan what they may say. They **do this just before falling asleep at night**. This film may run all night in their heads. Then, when they have the conversation the next day, they often feel the Eureka effect—a feeling that they've made a big leap forward.

Task 6: Affirmations

Another nice way to use self-talk is with affirmations. Affirmations are simply positive phrases about yourself and what you are doing, that make you feel good. You don't have to necessarily believe them to use them. They are simply things that you want to repeat to yourself. Often, without you noticing it, they begin to be true and they become a part of you. (The power of our words is so great that we become what we say, most of the time. Richard Bach says the very same thing in *Illusions*: 'Argue for your limitations and, sure enough, they're yours.')

Below are a few affirmations that you might want to experiment with. Say them to yourself three or four times a day for a while and notice what effect they have on you. Put a copy in your wallet. Or make up your own! Or do it with a song (see *Five Ways to Happiness!* in Appendix 5).

1. I really like speaking English – it's fun!
2. I'm learning more and more English every day.
3. I like talking to people.
4. Mistakes show I'm trying. I like mistakes.
5. Smiling is a great part of language.
6. I can speak English. I am an English speaker.
7. Learning English is a great adventure.

Self-talk is also **risk free**. Nobody can say you said it wrong, you can go as slow as you like, and you are free to say what you want. Nobody else hears you. Everywhere is a safe place to practise. And it will eventually make speaking out loud a lot easier. Listen to yourself saying something in your head in your foreign language **right now** and see how it feels.

Now make it a habit. Do yourself a favour
– do it regularly. And have fun!

Bach, R. 1977. *Illusions,* London: Pan.
Smith, F. 1983. *Essays Into Literacy,* London:
Heinemann pp 89—94.
Vygotsky, L. 1934/1962. *Language and Thought,*
MIT Press.

CHAPTER 5
A Teddy Bear in Your Ear!

CHAPTER 5
A Teddy Bear in Your Ear!

"Sing! You'll enjoy life more and live longer! And, who knows, you may even change the world."

Tanak Akay

Think about it first!
1. How can you use songs to increase your language learning?
2. How can you use a Walkman and increase your contact time with your target language?

A recent journal entry:

Riding my mountain bike to work this morning, going up a steep hill, I tried singing 'Cho Cho', a Japanese children's song about a butterfly who loves to play among the cherry blossoms. It amazed me for two reasons. First, I was surprised that I could easily remember it. I had heard it several times and even tried to memorize it about six months ago. I thought I had forgotten it. Secondly, I usually agonize getting to the top of that particular hill, while today I was at the top before I noticed it. Was my mind and body distracted by my singing the song? Or was it the bicycling that made remembering the song so easy? Or both of these?

We know that songs and music in language learning are fun. Songs are also good language-learning material for many other reasons (see box on p35). Some people, years after their language courses, only remember the songs they learned. Try a few of the suggestions below and see how they work for you. They all work for some people some of the time. Being a good learner means you can experiment with many different ways to learn, and find those that suit you.

Background Music (BGM)

Put on some BGM as you do other tasks. (Try it right now if you can. Use some BGM while reading about BGM.) Some students love to study with songs, and find that not only does it keep them awake but also they seem to learn two things at once.

Try recording the same favourite song three or four times in a row on the same CD, MD, cassette, or iPod playlist (or hit the repeat function on the latest technology). Try listening to it just before you go to sleep. (I don't know how much your brain works during the night, but mine dances up a storm!) BGM can increase your contact with your target language immensely. Even BGM without words can be used to put you into a good mood for study and give you energy.

Walkpeople with Teddy Bears in their Ears

Songs are naturally emotional, and we all need messages with affection. Songs are also risk-free: if you don't understand a song, the singer won't get angry with you, or embarrass you. In these two ways, songs are like a teddy bear in your ear, affectionate and risk-free. When we think of how we use a Walkman with earphones, the metaphor of the teddy bear in your ear comes alive. So, put a teddy bear in your ear and snuggle up with your imagination.

If you spend a lot of time travelling or waiting and

you want your time to be productive, invest in a teddy-bear-in-your-ear (buy a Walkman, iPod, or other such technology). Portable players will allow you to be in contact more with the target language. It will colour your empty time with sonic rainbows. Teddy bears are nice friends to have.

The Song Stuck in My Head Phenomenon

Have you ever had a piece of a song echoing in your head, which you can't stop? It may even be a song you don't like. But a line or two keeps repeating itself. This quite commonly happens with the last song you hear before leaving your home or car. Then you have some quiet (a pause) and the words go on repeating in your head. This common experience is greater when you sing along, and perhaps even more if you move, as when you are dancing and singing at a concert, disco or party. If you've ever been around young children who like a particular song, you also know that they sing along with the echoing in their head. (This may often drive you crazy before you can get away.)

So put on a song that you want to have echo in your brain, and play it just before leaving home. Don't worry about singing the whole song to yourself. Often it is just one or two lines that echo in your head.

Teachers can also help their students a lot by playing songs at the end of classes.

Shadowing/Echoing

Singing along with songs, out loud or in your head, is great practice. For songs you don't know yet, try shadowing and echoing, repeating as much as you can in the short pauses between phrases (see Chapter 4). You'll soon find yourself anticipating the lines and singing along.

Singing New Phrases

Try this: take a phrase you wish to learn in your foreign language, but don't quite have down smoothly. Say it to yourself once. Then say it again, adding a little tune to it – any tune that comes. Keep it simple. Then repeat the same phrase several times with that tune. If you do it enough times it may echo in your head on its own! Some people even write out longer dialogues and put them to music. This seems to work best when the words are put to a familiar tune, like 'Oh Susannah'.

Speaking Cassettes with BGM

I've asked French, German and Japanese friends to record a page or two of phrases that I want to learn, phrases I have collected or simply pages from a textbook. I tell them to repeat the phrase twice out loud **with feeling**, and then three times silently, before going on to the next one. I put music and songs on in the background as they record the phrases. The pauses leave time for my brain to process the sentence, and time for the BGM to entertain me. I occasionally make such cassettes for my students, and they report that they are useful and fun.

Finding Songs You Like at Your Level, and Getting Help from Others

More important than choosing songs at your language level is choosing songs that you like. If you like the songs, you'll spend more time with them. Of course it helps if you have the lyrics and go over them with someone who understands them. Once you understand the song, your repeated listenings will have more of a chance of making an impact on your learning. A native speaker or another learner can often loan you recordings of songs, and they can also explain the lyrics to you.

Recycling

One of the keys to learning with songs is taking small chunks and recycling them. So whatever words you are learning in the songs, USE THEM when you talk to others, or teach them to others. Transfer what you are learning in the songs to actual use.

Children's Songs

I started listening to Japanese children's songs a while ago. I was pleasantly surprised when I found I could ask friends and colleagues to explain the songs. They enjoy it, too; the most stern-looking university professor becomes a child again as he remembers how 'Zou-san' (Ms/Mr. Elephant) goes. Some children's songs come with motions, and these are especially useful. I find that even my university students enjoy English children's songs. Singing a song is like being a native speaker. It's hypnotic and healthy, like meditation. It makes you breathe!

The Best Songs to Learn

The best songs for you to try to learn are the ones you come into contact with through the people you meet. Even talking about songs becomes learning material. Most people love to talk about their favourite songs and to teach them to others. Experiment. Try lots of different songs and find those that suit you. And let the music hug you!

Smart Fun!
A Teddy Bear in Your Ear

1. Ask your friends what songs they listen to and learn from. Ask them if you can borrow the songs for a day.
2. Memorize a few songs from Appendix 5 of this book.
3. Listen to a song just before leaving home and try to sing it on the way to school.
4. Put the lyrics of a favourite song in your pocket. Look at it often and try to memorize the song. It's best if you have a friend who has agreed to hear you sing it. Better yet, agree to sing it together!

POP SONG MUSICAL RESEARCH

As part of my research in Switzerland in 1987, I analyzed the top 50 pop songs from the English hit parade, and found the following:

1. The songs have three main ingredients: *you*, *I*, and *love*. The *you* and *I* were almost never specified; that is, we didn't know who was being spoken to, or who was speaking. This means that usually you (yes, you reading this chapter) can place your own people, imagined or real, into these blanks.

2. In the songs there is almost no reference to *when* and *where*. That simply means that a song happens *whenever* and *wherever* you happen to hear it. Then it can take on the meanings of that place and time for you.

Test it. You can test 1 & 2 on yourself by remembering a favourite old song and seeing if specific times, places and people come to mind. Go ahead – try it right now. Think of a favourite song.

3. The songs run at about half the speed of normal speech. This is usually caused not so much by slower pronunciation as by longer pauses between phrases. These pauses, as we saw in the last chapter, may allow us to shadow and echo the phrases in our minds, if not actually out loud. The pauses also allow us time to make meaning or to search for what they mean to us.

4. The language in songs is simple. The reading level of the songs analyzed is about that of a child after four years of schooling. The simplicity of language is principally caused by massive repetition. The amount of repetition, of course, also makes it easier to shadow and echo.

So what?

What all this means is that songs are extremely well suited for language learning, and indeed everyone seems to learn them easily and quickly. (There are of course exceptions!) This is because most songs are simple, repetitive, fun, slow, short, and emotionally charged. They can add variety, play, and – yes – love to your language learning.

CHAPTER 6
Remember Your Memory ...
It's What You Make It

CHAPTER 6
Remember Your Memory ... It's What You Make It

OPPORTUNITYISNOWHERE? "No Where" or "Now Here"?
(You decide!)

Think about it first!
1. How do you remember new words?
2. What are the most effective ways to memorize information for a long time?

Reformulation Mary

Mary was a friend I had in college. Without studying much, she always got really good grades. It was a mystery to me. I wondered how she did it, so I began observing her more closely and asking her questions. This is what I found out:

1. I noticed Mary had the habit of telling everybody what her professors were lecturing about. After class she would tell her friends all about her professor's lecture. When she called home she would tell her mother what she was learning. When her boyfriend called, she would tell him. When she saw her grandmother she would tell her. Friends of hers said she even told her teddy bear.

2. Some of her classes were not really interesting to her, but still she wanted to learn and to make good grades. So she pretended (and then actually believed) that what her professors were saying was extremely interesting. Then she became excited about telling everybody about it. It was a game for her. By doing this, she was reformulating what the professor had said, teaching others, and making the material her own. She made it important, and then retold it as soon after hearing it as possible. She also made sure she retold it several times.

3. Because she did reformulation so much, and immediately after every class, she understood the material better. So she was also able to understand better what the professor said in the next class.

4. During class, she made mind-mapping notes with only a few words (see the mind map on p42). I suspect that she was also shadowing her teachers in order to understand more. When she didn't understand what the teacher said, she would take the bits she did understand and make her own ideas. And she would create a film in her head.

In contrast, most students, like me, only took notes and didn't really hear the ideas. Then we would put our notes away until we had a test. Later, when we tried to read our notes, we usually couldn't understand them. They were not complete, and we had not thought about the ideas for a long time. So because we couldn't really remember what the teacher had said the week before, each class seemed very different to us. It was frustrating. Yet, these classes were the same for Mary and for the rest of us.

After I found out how Mary did it, I tried it out. And it worked! It took a bit of practice and persistence (sometimes my cat didn't want to listen to me talk about anthropological linguistics).

YOU SEE, THE FUNDAMENTAL PRINCIPLES OF ANTHROPOLOGICAL LINGUISTICS LIE IN...

TEST

Test yourself. Read the following list of words once and then look away and write down as many as you can. Read them only once.

> book, tower, cloth, what, to, elephant, for, over, fly, fall, when

How did you do? Psychologists tell us that we tend to remember best the first, the last, and strange things. First, because that's the first impression. Last, because that is the most recent – and there is a pause afterwards, and that gives it time to echo. And strange things because they stand out from the ordinary. So if you remembered *book .... elephant .... when* from the above list, then you remembered what the psychologists had predicted you would remember.

However, each of us is different, and we can have different associations (connections) for each word. To someone who works every day in a *tower*, or with *cloth*, the associations with these words may have been richer and thus easier to remember. So things that are **important** and **familiar** are also easier to remember.

From Reformulation Mary I also learned that **frequency** has a big impact; do it often, and it's easier to remember. Mary also connected the material that she was learning to people she knew, by telling them about it. She remembered the different reactions of her friends and family. So the material became familiar, attached to people she knew and loved, in situations that were important to her. For all of us, new words become meaningful when we teach them to a close friend. That makes them easy to remember. By telling lots of people in brief moments, Mary also had lots of chances to explain the material in small chunks.

What is great about the human brain is that even if something is not first, strange, last, important, or familiar, the brain still has the power to **make that thing memorable**. The key is working smart – not necessarily hard – through **frequent recycling** of information in **meaningful** ways. So the thing to do is to organize our day and our mind to use new information frequently in meaningful ways – and that can be fun!

HELP YOUR MEMORY WORK WELL

1. Reformulate and recycle frequently

Decide on the things (stories, jokes, interesting ideas, descriptions of your classes, etc) that you can retell to many people. Set times to recycle new learning to yourself. Find people who you can talk to. Make appointments that you can't get out of. (I've found it's easy to ignore a book, but not meetings with people.)

2. Create lots of firsts and lasts

Study in short spurts. That way you will have lots of firsts and lasts, and the mind likes that. Studying for 10 minutes six times in a day with breaks is much better than cramming one hour straight.

3. Make things STRANGE

Houritsuka wa *himitsu* ga ooi (Lawyers have lots of secrets). In order to learn these two "h" words I imagined a bunch of lawyers whispering secrets into one another's ears. It may make little sense to anyone else, but it makes me laugh. That is what is important. Make an image that is strange or funny **to you** with whatever words you wish to remember. The stranger the image, the better for your memory.

4. Make things familiar

Connect the unfamiliar with the familiar. The lawyer who I imagine telling all the *himitsu* is my brother-in-law. Use the things that you are most familiar with to help you remember the new words.

5. Use story (episodic) memory

Stories are easy to remember. Strange stories are even easier. It doesn't even have to be true; just tell everyone it was a dream you had last night. By telling everybody, you will recycle it enough to get good at it. Each person you tell will help you make it even better: "Last night I had a strange dream; listen ..."

6. Make things important, fun and meaningful

Connect new information to things that are important for you. Reformulation Mary played a game in her head and connected all of her friends and family with her learning. Above all, make it fun. Then you'll do it a lot and learn a lot.

TYPES OF MEMORY

1. Sensory memory is what we first use to capture a sound. Shadowing (silently repeating what we hear) can help us do this and improve our ability to hold on to new words.

2. Short-term memory describes the brain's ability to pick up and register information for a few minutes to a few hours. When learning a language, we often meet new words or expressions, find out what they mean, and then forget them. Later, when we recognize them only vaguely, we tell ourselves, "But I learned that!" and become frustrated at our loss of time and hard work.

But working hard is not enough; we also need to work smart! Getting information from short-term into **long-term memory** depends principally upon:

1) what we first do with it when we get it, and
2) how frequently we meet it again.

3. Long-term memory is where the information is easy to use and recognize quickly. There are several other kinds of memories that can help us.

4. Episodic (story) memory involves remembering things because they happen in some order, like a story. The ability to see films in our heads and tie foreign words to events is a very powerful way to practise and learn language.

5. Skill memories are acquired through practice that turns into habits. Typical greetings and expressions are basic routines that we don't even think about after a while. It's to our advantage to learn as many routines as possible so that we can begin to interact and get people to speak to us. We can also use skill memories for our everyday routines, such as our morning washing and eating routines.

VAK

V is for visual, A is for auditory, and K is for kinaesthetic (body feeling). These form the basic material that your brain uses.

If you find a new word that you wish to remember, giving it a picture with sound and feeling will help your brain recall it better. Great memory experts usually have synaesthesia, in which they use all their senses to remember better. For them, a word calls forth a picture, a sound and a feeling, and perhaps even a taste and a smell. With many words you can actually make a movement which will help you to recall the words.

A last word – *Opportunity*

Perhaps the single most important thing that you can do to improve memory is to try out the above strategies often, so that they become automatic. If you give your brain the practice, the opportunity, to learn new strategies, it will pay you back richly. Learning how to do a sport or play a musical instrument takes practice; using your brain well also takes practice. Repetition is the mother of skill, meaningfulness is the father, and pleasure is the fertility rites. Go for it! Enjoy yourself!

Smart Fun!
Remember your memory

1. Make a list of people to whom you can tell what you have learned today. Then contact them and ask them if they would like to listen. Do it!

2. Experiment with drawing mind maps of your goals, your plans, your friends, etc. Then do a mind map during one of your lectures while you listen.

3. Memorize the mind map below, and then draw it and explain the different parts to others.

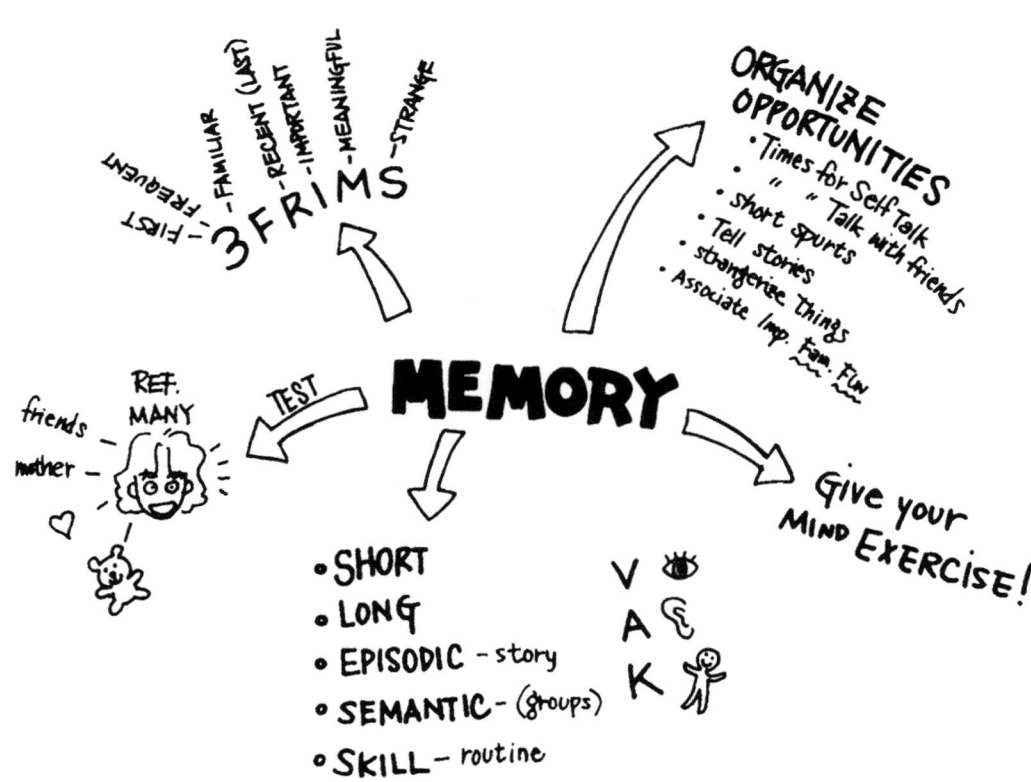

CHAPTER 7
Serious FUN!

CHAPTER 7
Serious FUN!

"Work? If you are not having fun, you are not doing it right! Every kid knows that!"

Tanak Akay

Think about it first!
1. How much do you enjoy learning?
2. How can you enjoy it more?

Research indicates that laughter does more than just temporarily cheer a person up. Laughter exercises the heart, lungs and adrenal glands, and stimulates the body's production of natural painkillers. Another tickling discovery: laughter can even help the learning process. Students' attention is increased when humor is interjected into the lessons. A fact which definitely results in a higher degree of learning retention! (O.F.E. Synd. 1985 *Gainesville Sun* March 20)

Play Consultants

Within the last few years, organisations such as IBM, AT&T, the US Army, the Bank of America, Monsanto, and even the IRS (the US tax collection agency) have hired play consultants to help their employees "**lighten up**" and enjoy their work: They have discovered that "**fun**" increases creativity and the ability to solve problems on the job (Millar, 1992). At Cornell University, researchers found that people who had just watched a short comedy film were more able to find creative solutions to puzzling problems. One play consultant in the San Francisco area organizes people into juggling teams and finds that afterwards they are more dynamically motivated to activate all their resources. (Ibid.)

What do chimpanzees and Einstein have in common?

In studying chimpanzees, the neuro-psychologist Donald Hebb concluded that the more playful animals were also the more intelligent ones (Milner, 1993).

Physicist Abraham Pais says the same of the two great physicists of our century, Einstein and Bohr: *Each had a lifelong boyish ... curiosity and pleasure in play. They took science very seriously, but to them it was ultimately a game* (1991).

Psychologists studying children have found that the playful ones are more resistant to frustration and giving up. It is because these children know how to make something into a game. The psychologists also concluded that play contributes to language acquisition, intelligence development, and well balanced development in children (Bruner et al. 1976).

If it's not fun, you're not doing it right.

It's logical that when you enjoy something you'll want to spend more time doing it. So if you really want to learn something like a language, which takes a good bit of time and energy – **make it fun**! When it's fun, you want to do it more. **You are in charge of your level of play.**

What most people don't realize is that the thing we are doing (for example, learning a language) can't in itself have qualities of being fun or not fun. It's *how we do it* and *how we think about it* that *make it fun*. And we can decide to think about what we are doing in a fun way or not. You are much more in charge than you think. To make it fun you can do two things:

1. Choose ways to study and learn that you find enjoyable.

2. Magicalize the ways you don't yet find enjoyable. Think about them in a fun way!

JUST DO IT!

CHOOSE FUN WAYS TO LEARN

Interact! You can work with other people and make studying more interesting. Put yourself in situations where you have to interact:

1. Ask people to teach you how to pay compliments in your target language, and then pay them.

2. Tell short, funny stories, the same ones, to everybody you meet.

3. Ask the time, ask survey questions (eg: "Please tell me five things you like.").

4. Make lots of dates to study with friends.

5. Play the game of talking in the language you're learning while eating meals.

6. Ask friends if they know the English word 'tickle'. If they don't know it, tickle them. It's fun, it's English, and you can blame it all on me!

Sing Songs! Songs are great tools that allow you to memorize things easily and with enjoyment. You can learn the ones you hear on the radio, or those that friends teach you, or you can get a collection of children's songs. You can also make up songs of your own with phrases that you want to remember. Teach them to friends. And remember, you can sing inside your head whenever you want to.

Be Active! If you simply sit reading and listening, you are not using all the possibilities. Find a friend who agrees to speak the language you are learning, then go bowling, shopping, walking, fishing, or skiing together. Meet conversation partners for lunch or for a drink.

Magicalize (don't smile too much when you read this)

There may be some things you have to do although you don't like doing them much. You may be wondering how you can change, and find yourself really enjoying such things. If you're willing to play along, it will be easy.

I'm going to ask you to play a game in your brain. If you just read this part without playing the game, it won't work, and you can say this chapter is useless, and you will be right. But when you do what I ask you to do, when you play along, you will find that your feelings towards the thing you don't like will actually change. It may help you to close your eyes when you do certain parts. You can also get a friend to guide you through the process.

CHAPTER 7: Serious FUN!

1. Decide on one thing that you feel you have to do for your studies, and that you don't like doing very much.

2. Now make a film in your mind in which you see yourself doing this thing in fast motion. Make the film last for just a few seconds. At the end of the film see yourself being completely satisfied with your work. Do this now, before you read further.

3. Now brighten the image, add some colours, add some of your favourite background music to it and run it fast forward again, seeing yourself doing whatever it is in fast motion. Again, see yourself being completely satisfied with yourself at the end.

4. Now say to yourself five times out loud, (or in your head), but either way with **passion**, "(Whatever it is) is fun!"

5. Now go inside yourself and check how your feelings have changed about the thing. How much better is it now?

After doing this, people usually report that they have more desire to do it, or at least their feeling about it is neutral. They can see more clearly what they need to do, and how to make it fun.

Different magic works for different people. Sometimes you need to change the location of your film, or repeat it a few more times. Experiment and see what your brain likes. *It is not the thing itself that is fun or not – it is the way we think about it.* Dare to play with your brain, and you will find that you can actually add more play and enjoyment in your learning. Einstein was playful enough to jump onto the end of a beam of light in his mind, and discover wonderful things. He dared to take a few risks and think differently.

We all have basically the same hardware in our brains as Einstein had. The difference is in how we use our brains. Working hard is not enough – we need to work smart. *Scientists believe that play is a higher evolutionary process that stimulates learning and well-being.* So, play plays an important role in the health and intelligence of monkeys, dolphins, and ... some humans. Maybe in you!

Bruner, J. S., Jolly, A., Sylva, K. (eds.) 1976. *Play – Its Role in Development and Evolution*, Penguin.
Millar, R. 1992. 'Lighten Up' *Sky Magazine*, Delta Airlines, Aug, pp 18—21.
Milner, Peter, 1993. 'The Mind of Donald O. Hebb' *Scientific American* 268(1) 104—109.
Pais, Abraham, 1991. 'Neils Bohr's Times', in *Physics, Philosophy, and Polity*, Oxford University Press (from a review in *Scientific American* 267(3) 1992).

CHAPTER 8
Learned Genkiness

CHAPTER 8
Learned Genkiness

"Every great and commanding moment in the annals of the world is the triumph of some enthusiasm."

Ralph Waldo Emerson

Question: What do you think could be the most important thing for success in language learning?
a) the textbook and materials
b) the method
c) the school
d) the teacher
e) the place
f) the people you are with.

Answer: All of these definitely affect your learning. But the most important thing is not in that list; it's reading these words – it's you, and your degree of genkiness*.

This is a new word in English that will be added to dictionaries in a few years.

Learned Helplessness

A scientist once put a rat in a cage. Then through the floor of the cage he gave electric shocks to the rat's feet. The rat jumped around the cage in great distress, looking for a way out. After a while, however, the rat learned that it couldn't avoid the shocks, no matter what it tried. So it simply sat in a corner of the cage, afraid and hopeless.

We know that people act somewhat like this too. Each of us will try many things to avoid or reduce pain. However, if we find our efforts have no result, we tend to passively accept the pain. The scientist wanted to show something more than this, so he put the same rat in another cage. This second cage had a bar in it that would stop the electric shock when pressed. However, the rat remained in the corner of the cage and simply accepted the shocks. It didn't try to search for a way to avoid the pain. *On the contrary, from its experience in the first cage the rat had learned to be helpless.*

According to psychologist Martin Seligman, some people learn to be helpless, like the rat, and so sometimes they don't try to improve the situation they are in. If you think this way, then you don't look for and, of course, you don't find any solutions. How does this happen? 'Seligman [thinks] … that one reason people fail to learn is because instead of receiving rewards for their efforts, they are punished for those otherwise adaptive responses, whether by design or accident.' (Taylor 1989, p185) In other words, the rat had tried to find a way out and its attempts had not been rewarded, so it had stopped trying. It carried this learning to the next cage and used this learned helplessness there, too.

Learned helplessness can be seen in many areas of our lives. For example, research has shown that people who *feel* they have no control in their jobs have low motivation and enthusiasm, do poorer quality work, and are more likely to get sick. Doctors have told us that when people feel they are not in control, they develop learned helplessness, which turns to hopelessness, which makes us open to disease. Siegel (1990) points out that although there are exterior and physiological reasons for disease, our emotions and attitudes determine how well we can defend ourselves. For example, one study reported that the

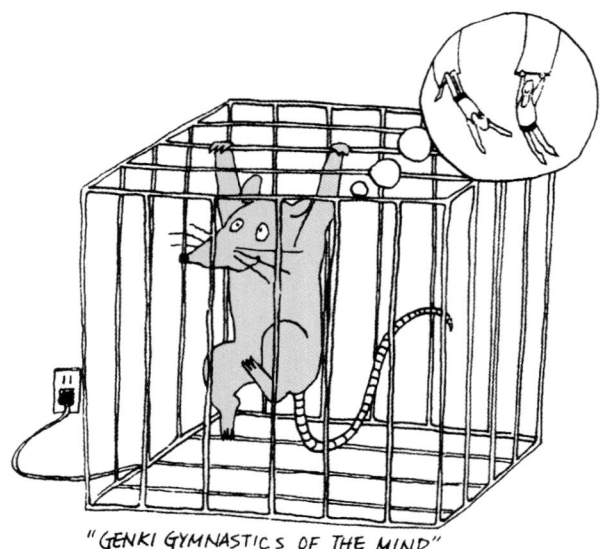

"GENKI GYMNASTICS OF THE MIND"

elderly in retirement homes were found to live longer when given plants to take care of. In other words they were given responsibility and control over a certain portion of their lives. *Taking control of our lives, and our learning, promotes positive learning and living.*

Teachers in schools might ask themselves how much control students are given over their own learning. Can students comment, suggest activities, offer materials? Are they invited to participate in the running of their lives in the classroom, or are they made to feel powerless? Are students only learning to do what the teacher says, and ignoring the boundless possibilities of what their minds are capable of?

Helpless Students

Even in the best of classrooms, I have seen students who automatically feel dominated by the teacher, school and materials, and who think that they have no choice. They are like the rat who has learned to be helpless in one situation and who carries this attitude to a new situation where there might be wonderful opportunities. So these students just don't see the opportunities. Helpless students think that outside factors determine how much they learn. They often blame outside

causes for poor results. They think that if they are given the right school, the right teacher, the right method, the right book, the right environment, the right etc, that they will learn easily and effectively. They expect those 'rights' to do the learning for them.

But you need to remember the part that you play. Having an 'I can' attitude is important. Put energy into learning. With your effort, anything can happen.

Proactive Students

When you are a proactive student, you go after what you want – you are always learning. For you, life is a feast of learning and food is everywhere. You are voraciously curious. You have realized that there's always something to learn in any situation. You find healthy food to eat everywhere. You search, you discover, you create. When you are faced by an overpowering teacher or test, you may submit externally, but you realize your mind is free to think anything you like and to learn anything you want to. You have learned to make your positive energy and your *genkiness* into a habit.

It is you yourself, and what you are doing with your own brain, that create learning. When you are a good language learner, you believe in your own control over the learning process. You do the things that you know work for you. You use classes and books as stimulation – but you realize that it's up to you whether you learn or not.

Steps to Learned Genkiness

People are amazing creatures. We can learn things almost anywhere, at any time, with anyone. So if we have learned to be helpless – then we can also learn to be in control. We can change, and this is great! Some students do well with almost any method and any teacher; believing in the method and the teacher may motivate you. However, the most important thing is to **believe in yourself, in your own capacity to learn**. This belief makes you stronger than the environment. So, how can you believe in your own capacity to learn and take charge?

1. Use your past learning as support for your belief in yourself. Take a moment and think back to a time when you learned how to do something easily and quickly, perhaps learning how to ride a bike, or any other task. Then list in your mind all the other things that you have learned, like your native language, how to drive, how to cook, how to play a certain sport or an instrument, etc. Now think of your language learning in the same way. Tell yourself that with the proper practice you'll be playing this language like you do your favourite sport or musical instrument, or maybe how you drive a car or cook a meal.

2. Look for the evidence that you have already begun to learn a lot of language. List the things you can already do and say with the language. Write down the fun times you have had when speaking the language. Notice that you can learn it and enjoy it as well. When you take charge, you can learn any way you want to, so you might as well make it fun!

3. Back up beliefs with some self-knowledge as well. How do you learn best? Think of the ways in which you learned things easily and quickly in the past. Take a moment to think about ways that you like to learn. Then think how you can use these ways in your language learning.

4. Decide what matters to you, **what is important for you to learn and what isn't important.** Not all the literature and expressions in a language are necessarily useful for you. Notice the things you can use. Notice what you can ignore. Select what you want to learn.

5. Fix some goals and make a programme. Decide what you can do, decide what you want to do, set some goals, make some plans, write them down, mark your calendar, make a list, note it in a journal. And it's okay to get excited about it!

6. Next, of course, **act upon this knowledge**; do what you have planned. If it doesn't work right away, keep doing it. If it doesn't work after a while, then try something else. (For example, I know I like to learn with people, so I act on this knowledge by setting up as many appointments as I can. If it doesn't work with one partner, I find others.)

7. When you start to see your results, be flexible and **adjust what you are doing to make your learning even more effective.** What if you really could see yourself learning easily and smoothly and enjoyably? At the same time as you're visualizing this, notice how you are learning, where, and with whom. Then you can do it in the real world. You are in charge. You have a lot of options. Just do it!

In conclusion, *you are a natural learning machine*. The question is how you can continue to open yourself up to even more of your potential.

Background information in this chapter was first read in *Positive Illusions* (by Dr. Shelly E. Taylor, New York: Basic Books 1989), *Love Medicine & Miracles* (by Dr. Bernie S. Siegel, Harper & Row 1990), *The Self–Healing Personality* (by Dr. Howard S. Friedman, Penguin 1991) and *Learned Optimism* (M. Seligman, New York: Pocket Books 1990).

CHAPTER 9
The Joys of Friendly Watching and Upside Downing Time

CHAPTER 9
The Joys of Friendly Watching and Upside Downing Time

"The only way to change the future is to change the present. Whatever you are doing now is creating your future."

Mits

Think about it first!
1. How do you remember you want to be happy and to study?
2. How can you remind yourself?

It's a great idea to wear your watch upside down. I watch my watch many many times every day, so I can be happy many times!! (Now is the best time to be happy!) I'll keep wearing the English reminder watch!? (From a student journal by Yuki Mizuta)

In my classes, I ask students to conduct a little experiment with me. I ask them to take off their watches and to put them back on **upside down,** and to keep them that way for at least a week. When you do this, you can observe several interesting things:

1. When you've worn your watch upside down for a full week, you will have no trouble telling the time upside down by the end of that week. You will also notice that you can read everyone else's watch. You will be learning a new perspective, breaking routine and learning a new skill. This skill can be very useful, for example when you are with someone in a café. It might be rude to look at your own watch because they might think you are in a hurry and don't want to talk to them. So, instead, you look at *their* watch, which is upside down for you. It's simple!

2. I bet that not more than two people will even notice that your watch is upside down. When others do notice, you can give several responses, such as, "That's the way it was when I first bought it!" or, "I put on the watch that way on purpose so that other people could read it more easily. It's called a *friendly watch* – it's worn that way for the convenience of others."

3. Each time during the week that you look at your watch, you will notice that it is upside down and you will remember your crazy English teacher who always says, "Now is the best time to be happy." In class I ask students to repeat the sentence several times with me, and I tell them they are to say the phrase to themselves every time they look at their watch during the week. (If you are learning another language, translate the phrase.) It's a reminder to be happy, too!

4. Finally, when you look at your watch periodically and say "Now is the best time to ...", you are reminded also that you want to learn more. You can describe in self-talk what is around you at the time, you can review your new vocabulary and idioms in your mind, or you can plan what you will do in your target language. *The essence of effective learning is regular and frequent review of the things that you are learning in many different contexts.* If students meet new words only in a classroom or in an exercise book, all that knowledge is usually available in only

those contexts. Using the upside-down watch makes language learning available anywhere, any time, and deepens the learning process. The upside-down watch reminds you that you can review at any time.

In class, I explain all these reasons to my students right away, and then I ask them to ask each other what time it is, and to answer each other with, "Now is the best time to be happy!" Every 10 minutes or so during the rest of the lesson I ask them to ask their partners again. For homework that week they must often ask their classmates what time it is.

What happens most of the time?
A few students don't remember because they are not flexible enough. They may put their watches back on the wrong way after a bath. A few others give up because they feel bothered by a little inconvenience, and they are not interested in learning something new. Some are afraid of being embarrassed when others notice their watches. But for a great many students, it loosens their grip on conventional ways of thinking. They can question with a new perspective what's right and wrong. *A watch turned the other way is not wrong - it's only different. And being different sometimes has a lot of advantages.*

Students also discover that time is given more importance than it deserves. They notice how often they look at their watches and how controlled they are by a schedule. They start looking at time differently.

However, the biggest boost is simply in your ability to control your own mood and emotions. Many students tell me that simply by looking at their watch they realize that **NOW IS THE BEST TIME TO BE HAPPY!** We tend to get caught up in our daily routines, and we forget to care about how we feel. When, every time you look at your watch, you take a moment to remind yourself to **enjoy right now**, it happens. *Right now* doesn't stay long - and before we know it, it's gone!

Being different sometimes has a lot of advantages.

This activity is a measure of your willingness to experiment and try different ways to learn, a measure of your persistence in exploring and adventuring with your brain, a measure of your willingness to put up with a bit of confusion long enough to learn something new. It shows your willingness to stand out and be different, and to make what others might call a stupid mistake. Some students continue learning from their watch for years.

Variations
After the upside-down watch has become commonplace, a variation that works well is to put your watch on your other wrist; this will further disorient you for a while. (Artist Kaori Miura originally suggested this to me.)
When this, too, has become commonplace, switch your watch back to

the original position, and notice how the original position is now strange and you have to get used to it again. This is usually what happens, so you can understand more deeply the arbitrary nature of our habits.

Internationally watching watches

When I travel internationally I play the game with myself not by changing my watch but by simply figuring out in my mind the time, adding seven or so hours to what my upside-down watch **says**. (By the way, what does your watch's voice sound like?) After a few days, doing this becomes automatic, so that when I get back to Japan I am confused again at first because I don't have to add or subtract any hours. And then I have to recondition myself not to add what isn't there. Conclusion: once we learn complicated ways to think about our environment, it takes some effort to learn how to be simple again.

And then there are those of us who regularly put our watches 5 or 10 minutes fast so we can relax, thinking we are always ahead of everyone else – until we have to rush to catch up with our overestimated aheadness.

Smart Fun!

? sdrawkcab siht daer uoy naC

1. You might turn your alarm clock upside down, or your wall clock, or your name, or …

2. What else can you turn upside down and learn from? A "wab" maybe?

3. Consider other alternative upside downing. Walk to school a different way, eat dessert first, wear your pyjamas to school, brush your teeth with your other hand. What other ways can you think of to mix up your routine?

4. Put 'It's time to be happy' on your mobile.

The Joys Friendly Watching and Upside Downing Time

CHAPTER 10

Just You and Your Walkman*
EARly Environmental Engineering
Giving Yourself What You Need

CHAPTER 10
Just You and Your Walkman*

> ### "That so few now dare to be eccentric marks the chief danger of our time."
> John Stuart Mill

Think about it first!
1. How can you shape your environment to get more of the learning you want?
2. What tools could you use to increase your learning?

In Switzerland we used to joke about Walter who always walked around school with his Walkman – we called it his life-support system (comparing him to the astronauts). Then in exams he got all the top grades while the other students were barely surviving. We found out that what he was always listening to were classes that he had recorded. He also edited them and added his own information. He became fluent in German after two years through making his own conversation tapes and listening to them. While other students were all red-eyed from reading and reviewing their notes, Walter walked through the town and the mountains listening to his Walkman. While others waited for their environment to give the right language (which it seldom did!), Walter made his environment give him what he needed.

If I had my way every language student would have a Walkman as standard equipment for school. However, 50% of all they listened to would be in their own voice, giving themselves the new vocabulary and expressions in meaningful messages that they know they need at the level they are at. Students who do this regularly will speed up their language learning immensely! (Tim Murphey's notes to himself, Nov. 1991)

When I see somebody with a Walkman somewhere, I often have the desire to take their earphone out of their ear and find out what they are listening to, what they are learning, what kind of brain food they are secretly feeding themselves. Of course, I know that some are listening to music, and this is good for us, too. However, a good number are learning wonderful things with language cassettes and really using their time wisely. When I see them, I don't want to be left out, and I regret that I left my Walkman at home.

As people who want to learn language, we get a lot of different language offered to us – from books, teachers and the environment. Some of it is useful, some of it is easy, some of it is way beyond us. My belief is that *you know which words you can understand and possibly learn when you see them.*

Therefore, I think that *you are the best person to choose things for yourself to learn.*

Most people know this already and make a selection of some kind. After this selection of useful things to learn, the big question is: **How do you recycle it enough to really learn it?** Babies learning their first language have loving mothers who know the baby's level and use the words that the baby knows and is learning, over and over, again and again. As adults, we don't usually have such ideal natural language recycling machines to help us. But with your Walkman you can make them.

If you wait for your environment to supply the words you need, you may have a very long wait ahead of you. But as a proactive language learner, *you can decide what you want to learn and then organize your environment for your learning.* You can take control of your learning, and at the same time make it fun and meaningful. How can you do it? Try out the recipe below, and remember: good cooks sometimes have to try a new recipe a few times before they get it right.

Step 1: Collecting language to be learned

It's simple. You probably already do this. Collect the things you really want to learn. Make a list. Not too long a list. Also, for the purpose of the tapes you will make, you might ask the following questions for each item:

1. Is this something I can actually imagine myself saying to someone?

2. Is this short enough and easy to understand?

3. Is this common in everyday conversation for native speakers?

Cut out of your list the items that don't correspond to these requirements. As a busy and effective language learner you might want to spend most of your time learning those things that will be **maximally useful** to you. That means choosing things that are within your zone of proximal development, the approximate level that you are at. (Vygotsky 1934/1962) If you reach too high, you only grab frustration; too low, and you grab boredom. Go for those things that are within your reach and that you can put to use.

Step 2: BGM and You

Choose some of your favourite relaxing or stimulating background music, whether instrumental or songs. If songs, it's probably better for them to be in the target language.

EXCHANGING BRAINFOOD

Step 3: Record the list yourself

Turn on your BGM, and record yourself saying the items into another recorder, in a nice, soothing voice. After recording for a minute or two, it's a good idea to stop and listen to what you have done and see if you would like the background music softer or louder and if you need to adjust the quality of your voice.

Some people like to repeat one item several times, and some leave pauses between the items so that they can also enjoy the BGM. Some also like to whisper the translation if it's something new. Some people tell stories or routines, describe things, or read from their journals or books. Some people interview other people. Whatever you do, you can have fun with it.

Make short recordings, just 10—30

minutes, with a small amount of new material that can be repeated often (preferably on a player that keeps the tape playing one side after another, endlessly). Experiment and see what suits you best. Some people mix songs and speaking, and surprise themselves.

Step 4: Listen often

Listen to your recording often. Favourite times are usually before going to bed; when you wake up and as you prepare to leave for school or work; on the tube, train, or bus; while walking to work; during your lunch break, etc. When you have recorded music you like and recorded your voice in a pleasing manner, the programme should be pleasant whether or not you pay any attention to the language. **When it's pleasant, you feel like listening more often.**

More Options

Some students make lots of **different recordings** for different topics. So if they regularly play tennis, they might listen to their tennis vocabulary just before going to the court.

Some students **trade recordings with other students** and learn the useful things the others are learning.

> You are in the best position to judge what you need. Why not give it to yourself?

Some students record **jokes, sayings, cheers, chants, idioms; some read short quotes, articles, opinions, song lyrics**, some pretend to interview famous people, etc. The list is limitless.

Many students make written **study-lists for tests.** When you turn these into audio tapes, you increase the amount of potential contact time immensely. Our eyes get weary. Our ears don't. We can listen and study with our eyes closed!

Audio recordings also work for **learning other material** that you want to have immediately to hand: dates in history, authors and themes, chemistry formulae, etc.

You can also, like Walter, **record your classes**; edit the recording down to the really good parts that you need to remember, and then re-listen to it often before you do tests or you write papers. You should ask permission, of course, but teachers are usually pleased that their students want to record them.

Why does it work?

We can think about learning as having three steps. First we REGISTER information in our short-term memory. If we have time and it is significant enough we try to RETAIN it (keep it). Then if we meet the new information often, it takes on depth. This means that we can recognize it later, and we can also freely RECALL it (say it when we want to).

Most language learners find out very quickly that a lot of information is hard to even register, and because it goes by so fast it is difficult to retain. Then, because it is not recycled (not heard again) often enough, it has little chance of being recognized later, and even less chance of being freely recalled. That is where the Walkman comes in.

When you record a teacher speaking, you REGISTER the information on something, like a Walkman, that can help your brain. When you listen to the Walkman later, you are recycling the information. This gives your brain enough quality input to build RETENTION and RECALL capabilities.

So, recording classes gives your short-term memory a backup. Selecting (editing) the valuable input later allows you to choose the brain food that is really useful for you to learn. Playing this high-quality selected input to yourself later gives your brain the time and repetitions that it needs to process the language and store it in long-term memory.

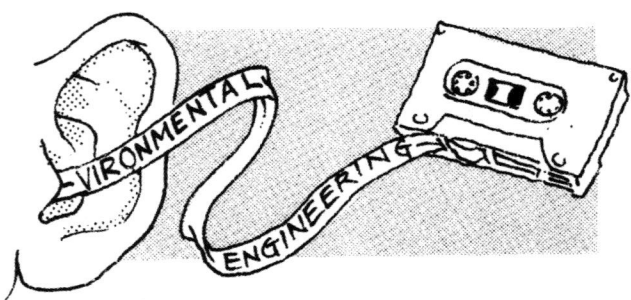

Entrance Exams and Listening Comprehension

Many ministries of education are encouraging teachers to teach some form of listening comprehension. Many university entrance exams are also changing, even if slowly, to reflect this shift in emphasis. High school teachers who are often hesitant to speak English in class can use the ideas in this chapter to help stimulate more listening comprehension in the educational system. Parents and students, however, don't have to wait for teachers to suggest working smart with a Walkman. Nobody ever told Walter to do it. He just wanted to learn effectively with as little effort as possible. He wanted to work smart. He was an EARly bird, an EARly environmental engineer – or should we say an EARly EARnvironmental EnginEAR?

Vygotsky, Lev 1934/1962 *Thought and Language* Cambridge, MA: MIT Press.

(*. The term Walkman is used generically and does not refer to any specific producer of recording devices.)

CHAPTER 11
Everyone's a Juggler!

CHAPTER 11
Everyone's a Juggler!

"I am not afraid to fail ... but I will not accept not trying."
Michael Jordan

Think about it first!
1. What might juggling have to do with language learning?

Today we learned juggling, but I'm not sure what Mr. Murphey wants us to do. It can't be only learning juggling. I thought it in two ways. First, Mr. Murphey wants us to learn English used in learning juggling. Second, he wants us to learn that there are also some steps in learning English. I don't know which of these or another Mr. Murphey wants us to learn, but it's good to get used to many things. (Satoru)

Communicative juggling

Imagine for a moment walking down the halls of a university building. As you pass by one class you see 40 students throwing juggling balls up in the air, getting very excited as they succeed, and shouting, "I did it!" I admit that I too would be curious for an explanation.

For several years I have used juggling as a learning device for my students. I suppose other professors and students occasionally think it's a bit odd. At the end of a class, I sometimes even take my students to the green area of our campus or out into the main street for some juggling.

We went out and tried to juggle. It was wonderful. I love it! I was not ashamed to be seen by passerbyes at all. There was no time for thinking about such a thing. I was absorbed in juggling and speaking English. This class teaches me a lot of things! (Etsuko)

Many students inevitably get hooked on juggling and borrow the balls for a while. I loan them on the condition that they have to teach others how to juggle, do it in English, and write a short report about it.

I played with the juggling balls almost every day [during the summer]. I taught 5 people how to juggle. Of course in English. I taught my father, sister, mother, grandmother and one of my friends who lives in Hiroshima. Now my sister plays it better than me. To my surprise my grandmother became a juggler after practicing for 15 minutes. (Cherry)

Learning to juggle teaches you that you can learn when you continue to try:

Juggling taught me that the more I exercise the better I can do. (Chiho)

It also allows you to examine your learning beliefs, emotions, and strategies. It illustrates the roller coaster of learning as you progress and seem to go backwards sometimes. It increases your self-esteem, which makes learning other things easier. It's an interesting way to observe how our attitudes interact with our brains and bodies.

To our surprise, we dropped the ball as soon as we became conscious and tried to juggle very well. It was interesting! (Sanae)

Juggling takes the theory of learning out of the textbooks and puts it in your hands, in front of your eyes, in your voice as you triumphantly shout, "I DID IT!"

Learning universals

There are certain things that are present in learning anything, whether it's a language, juggling, or pancake-tossing.

These are 1) beliefs, 2) emotions, 3) strategies, 4) a learner's level, and 5) small steps and chunks that allow easier learning. I'm sure there are more, but let's just juggle with these for a moment and see where they take us.

Beliefs

I remember the first class when we started juggling. I couldn't believe that I would be able to juggle, at first. I couldn't believe the power of beliefs, at first. But I do believe it now … I'm trying to be more active and to believe in my possibility. (Aki)

You have a set of **beliefs** about your ability to learn something. Very often, what you expect is what you get. Much has been written in the medical fields about self-fulfilling prophecies: whatever you believe has a way of coming true when you start to expect it, and your brain does its best to respond and gets you to do certain things that will help you do it.

Beliefs have been researched well enough now to show that they do contribute greatly to the results we get. If right now you were going to learn something you had never done before, like juggling, or flying a rocket into space, what would your reaction be? Listen to your self-talk for a moment. Feel what you would feel. Write it down and think about it.

Emotions

You are always in some **emotional state**.

When you are excited about learning, this will usually help you. Our emotions can change a lot.

The important question is, can you change them yourself to help you learn more easily? I think you can. For example, right now think of a time when you were very curious about something and learned it well. Maybe it was riding a bicycle, doing a sport, or learning to drive. Remember how excited you were about it! How do you feel now when you remember that success? The chances are that even thinking of that time gets you excited and gives you confidence that you can learn new things. And this makes actually learning them much easier (self-fulfilling).

Strategies

Your particular **strategies**, the ways you choose to learn, will also affect how fast you learn and with what results. Some people like to learn in a certain way, and when teachers teach that way learning is easier. However, when you are open to trying learning in many different ways, you increase your chances of learning quickly and learning many things from many people.

You may have a preference for information that is visual (pictures), auditory (talk and music and sounds), or kinaesthetic (body movement and feelings). Of course, each of us uses all of them to different degrees. Little children typically learn a lot by actually doing things in rich experiences; they love to move their bodies, look at picture books, and sing songs. Later in school, we mostly just read and listen to words. When you can make a film in your mind of the information and you tell other people about what you are learning, you turn this dry-word information into musical rainbows of dance. If you were going to learn to juggle just now, would you want an explanation (auditory), would you like someone to show you (visual), or would you like to take the balls and try it (kinaesthetic)?

Learning level

You have an individual **level** of ability for whatever you try to learn. When the materials, method, and learning partners can approximately **adjust** to that level, it's easier for you to learn. In a classroom, it's hard for one teacher to adjust to all the different levels at the same time. So people working together in pairs usually do a much better job than any one teacher can do with many students. Advanced students working with less advanced can still learn new things, and, through teaching, learn the old things even more deeply.

Steps

Creating small steps, or chunks, of material can help you learn faster. For some learners the steps and chunks need to be smaller. Other learners can jump steps and take bigger chunks. Time needed on certain steps will usually vary among students. Of course, in juggling it seems to be self-evident that you start with one ball, then go on to two, and then on to three. There is also the possibility of going back to earlier steps when you need to be more sure of yourself.

'Chunking' is often left to the teacher. But it's **you who are the better judge of what**

size chunk you can handle, how fast you can go, and when you need to go back to previous steps. After all, the balls are in your hands, the language comes out of your mouth, and the language is in your brain.

Self-confidence

Thanks to today's juggle, I could have confidence for learning anything. So I think I will learn English with this confidence after this. (Naoyuki)

Succeeding in juggling usually gives you a Eureka! effect: "I did it!" It increases your self-confidence immensely. This of course carries over to other things you are learning. Juggling also allows you to notice other learning phenomena, such as the roller coaster of progress (see Chapter 1), the inevitable ups and downs that we experience in learning anything. For students who know *otedama*, the traditional Japanese bean-bag game that's similar to juggling, learning true juggling is really interesting, because it demands a bit of reprogramming to overcome the interference from previous learning.

Juggling Manga

As you look over the juggling manga (see p166), work out what beliefs, emotions and strategies are shown. Then decide which of the two stereotypical characters you more closely resemble, and which of them you would like to resemble. In the last frame the two boys are doing the same thing with the balls; they each throw them around twice. But whereas the boy on the top calls what he does 'success', the boy on the bottom calls what he does 'failure'. Which do you think would be more productive for future learning? It's fascinating!

I leave you with one last student quote:
We confirmed that BELIEFS are important for us to learn anything. Then we did juggling with each other actually. We

missed again and again but kept trying. We are believers. We reached not perfect but "SUCCESS"! (Mayu)

In my mind, if you are trying you are succeeding; you are a juggler as soon as you dare to try.

N.B. A version of this chapter appeared in *Jugglers' World*, Spring 1995, pp38—39

CHAPTER 12
Brain Play I: On Second Thought

CHAPTER 12
Brain Play I: On Second Thought

"In the midst of winter, I finally discovered within me an invincible summer."

Albert Camus

Think about it first!
1. What makes you happy or sad?
2. Can you make yourself feel different ways about the same thing? Can you like it and not like it?
3. What's the connection between your thoughts, your feelings, and your behaviour?

Fascinatingly Boring!

When I was a ten-year-old, I once confessed to my Dad, "School is boring."

He said, "What?" - acting as though he hadn't heard me. So I repeated, "School is boring!"

His eyebrows rose with a concerned and slow, "I see." With his hand on his chin, he stared into space for a moment, and then as if struck by a meteor from inner space, he suddenly shot back, "How many kids in your class?"

"About 30."

"And how old are they?"

"They're ten, like me."

"Thirty kids, all ten years old – wow!" and he stared into space as if some miracle had happened.

"What?" I begged. I couldn't imagine what was so magical about 30 ten-year-olds.

"Well," he said, pausing just long enough to make sure I was interested, "30 kids, each ten years old, that makes **300 years** total. Three hundred years' worth of living, in the same room, at the same time. Each person so different, with thoughts and beliefs and ideas. I mean, just trying to imagine what each one had

for breakfast is amazing! Or what each one is thinking at any one moment! Imagine if thoughts could be heard, wow, you could hear 30 thoughts at the same time! I wonder what secrets they all have. I wonder what they dream at night?"

At the ripe old age of ten I'd had ten years experience of living with my Dad. So I already knew he was a little different from other Dads. My response was to roll my eyes toward the sky and walk away.

But the next day in school, I couldn't keep from wondering what all my classmates had had for breakfast, what they had dreamed about the night before, what made them the way they were, and what they were thinking about when the teacher was talking. School didn't change, but my perspective and behaviour did. Suddenly going to school was more like going to the zoo. Everything became fascinating.

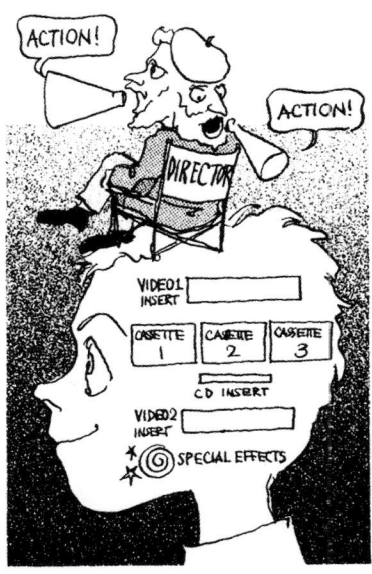

A	→	B	→	C
Something happens		**We think something**		**We feel something**
Rain		I'm going to get wet		already uncomfortable
		I'll be late		worried
		Dangerous to drive		frightened
		I can't play tennis		depressed
		The car is getting washed		relieved
		The plants all like it		pleased
		Snow in the mountains		happy
		Fell in love in the rain		warmly nostalgic

Rain

Some people will tell you that rain makes them feel bad. It's not true. The rain can't do that by itself. Only their thinking about the rain can do that. It's what they think about the rain that makes them feel bad. I have a friend who says she loves the rain. She imagines how the flowers and trees and plants feel being washed, watered, and caressed. She imagines how clean it makes the roads and buildings. In winter, she imagines the rain is snow in the mountains and she dreams of going skiing. She remembers a time when she fell in love with someone in the rain. Some people think she's crazy. I think she's learned how to control her brain and to make herself happy on rainy days. But even so, it's still not the rain that makes my friend happy, but her thinking (see box above). With small things, what happens (A) doesn't in itself make you feel something (C). It's your thinking (B) about what happens that causes those emotions (C). Once you realize that there are different ways to think about the same thing, then you've got choice.

It makes more sense to **choose what you think according to the context** rather than simply always feeling one particular way when something happens. In the example above, it is probably a good idea to feel a bit frightened when driving in the rain because your resulting behaviour will be to drive more carefully. If you were driving in the rain and thinking about an old love affair it would be dangerous – but such thoughts while sitting in a café watching the rain can be wonderful, and safe!

The way we talk sometimes hides our beliefs and opinions (B). So when we begin to question such phrases as 'The weather depresses me' or 'He didn't say hello so he doesn't like me', then we can see there are alternatives. When you see alternative thoughts, you can make a choice, and this will have an impact upon your emotions, which in turn determines your behaviour.

Now I wouldn't want to suggest that we can control all our thinking, all our emotions, and all our behaviour. But we do know there is a lot that we already do

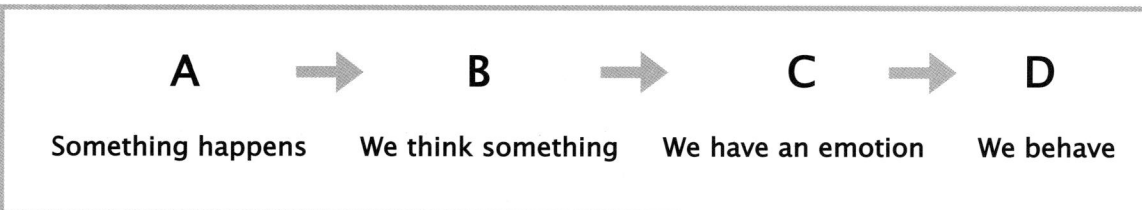

A	→	B	→	C	→	D
Something happens		**We think something**		**We have an emotion**		**We behave**

CHAPTER 12: Brain Play I: On Second Thought

control. And we also know that some people use their brains in amazingly creative ways to write books, make films, and be happy, so the chances are that there's a lot more that we can control.

So how about language-learning?

What do you think about language classes, talking to native speakers, talking to non-natives in the target language, studying alone, spelling and writing? If you feel as though you should be doing more of something and you never get around to it, it could be that you have some unconscious thoughts that you can explore, as in the list below.

If we compare our brains to a Mercedes-Benz, most of us haven't got out of first gear yet – or we don't even know that it has got other gears! When we want to, we can learn to do amazing things and use our brains much more effectively. I suspect I use my brain the same way as I use my new Apple Mac computer. I'm still using it as a simple word processor when it's capable of much, much more. Sometimes just playing around with it, I find out some wonderful things that it can do. If you are curious about your brain, play with it and see what it can do for you.

Playing with your brain

In these sequences, stop after reading each point to do what it asks.

1. Write down something that you have to do but you don't like doing (A).
   Then write down the usual emotion (C1) that you feel when you do this thing.
   Then write down the opposite emotion (C2).
   Next, what thoughts do you have to think to produce each of those two different emotions? (Insert these as B1 and B2.)
   Then consider what different types of behaviour the thoughts and emotions generate (D1 and D2).

2. Get a friend to tell you of something they don't like doing but have to do, for example travelling to school. This may be a thing that you agree with completely.
   Pretend (acting sincerely) that this really has a lot of merit, that it has very good points, is even fun! (Eg on your way to school, you can review your lessons, talk to friends, listen to music, etc.) Find the good points and tell your friend about them in an enthusiastic way. (Notice how when you act sincerely, you, the actor, may actually start to believe what is pretended.)

3. Think of a pleasant, peaceful place. Imagine that you are there right now. Take a deep breath and smell what is there.
   See the colours more brightly.
   Hear the sounds more intensely.
   Make the picture twice as big.
   Now make it as big as life.
   Give that feeling a name like 'passionate peacefulness'.
   Say it three times in a pleasing way

A	→	B	→	C	→	D
Something happens Language Learning		**We think something** It's too hard It's okay *It's fun*		**We have an emotion** depressed lackadaisical *happy*		**We behave** don't feel like studying study for tests only *interact with others*

while still seeing the picture.

Write the name down on a piece of paper and tape it to your bathroom mirror.

Notice what happens when you see it next.

Where would it be useful to put it so that you see it when you need it?

4. Pick a word you want to learn.

Visualize it appearing in front of you.

Think of someone you like very much.

Visualize that person, making them larger than life.

See the person holding the word and doing something with it as you hear that person saying it.

5. Think of two things you love doing.

Make a picture of each one.

Now put the first one on your own video player in your brain and let it come alive.

Make it bigger.

Then let the second picture zoom in from somewhere and watch it for a moment.

Then combine the two, side by side or some other way, and watch them both at the same time.

Then think of a third thing and put that somewhere in the collage of films.

Now, what are the different sounds you hear and feelings you feel?

6. Think of a speaker who you wish to speak like.

See the posture of this person and imitate it now, and see yourself in a parallel film looking just like the person.

In your mind, rerun a film of the person, see what things you notice and copy these over to the film of yourself. You may notice gestures, a certain tone of voice or speed of talking, a certain confidence, some beliefs that seem to be present, a kind of gentleness, a way of expressing oneself.

Copy all this over to the film of yourself and adjust it until it feels good.

Then, for a few days at least, act like this person when you're talking. Notice what happens as your internal film projects the characteristics of this other person inside yourself.

Swimming-pool hypnosis

I used to find swimming in a pool rather boring, in addition to being hard work. But swimming in the mountain lakes in Switzerland is my idea of breath-taking beauty. So the other night while swimming in the pool, I recited some of the Japanese words I was learning.

Soon the words came automatically as I put myself into a kind of trance. I lost count of how many lengths I was swimming. When I stopped, I realized that I had swum twice as long as I had planned and I hadn't even noticed – and the next day my arms were really sore! So the next time I experimented with seeing my word on the bottom of the pool. That slowed me down to look more closely. It was amazing!

The point is that you have a brain with its own internal sensorama with multivox sound and video editing potential. You can take what the environment offers you and select pieces to repeat, increase, colour, etc. Any special effects you see, you can duplicate, and you can even do more. We already do this naturally. On the negative side we call them phobias, obsessions, and traumas, and on the positive side we call them Einsteins, Disneys, and Mozarts. Or, as Kurt Vonnegut has said, "We are what we pretend to be, so we must be careful about what we pretend to be." (*Mother Night*, Kurt Vonnegut)

CHAPTER 13
Brain Play II: Fun with Junkthought

CHAPTER 13
Brain Play II: Fun with Junkthought

*"It is not enough to have a good mind.
The main thing is to use it well."*

René Descartes, 1637

"The greatest discovery of my generation is that human beings can alter their lives by altering their attitudes of mind."

William James, c 1890

Think about it first!
1. How much do you think with facts and with beliefs?
2. How do you talk to yourself inside your head?
3. Can you be your own best friend?
4. Are you interested in being able to help yourself think more rationally and control your feelings more so that you can be happier?

In the last chapter, I invited you to consider the possibility that our feelings are often caused by what we think. I also said that we can learn to think other things when we want to. Or in the words of Aldous Huxley (c 1939): 'Experience is not what happens to you; it is what you do with what happens to you.'

The new mind-body science of *psychoneuro*immu*no*logy (to get your tongue around it, stress the italic syllables) is telling us that our thoughts stimulate the neurology in our brains to trigger the release of chemicals and physiological processes. These can affect the ability of our immune system to defend us. This is actually the way mental stress can create bodily disease (dis-ease, uncomfortableness), and how things like meditation, exercise, and relaxation can refresh us. Of course, heredity, environment, and behaviour also influence our health. However, the way you think may often counterbalance negative influences from these other areas, and prolong life and enrich learning.

So what we feed our minds also nourishes our bodies. Becoming aware of what we usually put in our minds, and learning to control it, can make us not only healthier but also happier and better learners. If you often, or even just sometimes, get frustrated, depressed, upset or angry for no apparent reason, then it may be time to look at what you are thinking. To do this, we can recognize when a thought might be a junkthought that produces negative stress.

So how do you train yourself to recognize such thoughts? For our purpose here, we can divide thoughts into three categories: facts, rational beliefs, and irrational beliefs:

Facts are usually accepted by almost everyone as true: 'Cars are made in Japan.'

A **rational** belief is an opinion that is accepted by a lot of people, but could also be questioned by some, for example: 'Japanese cars are great.'

An <u>ir</u>**rational** belief is usually an extreme belief and may anger some people and cause problems for ourselves if we insist on it; for example: 'Japanese cars are the **only** good cars in the world and if you don't own one you must be crazy.'

Irrational beliefs = Junkthoughts

Jill Anderson (1981) highlights four kinds of irrational thinking that she calls junkthoughts: over-generalizing, catastrophizing, copping out and demanding. There are often key words that let you know when these occur.

Over-generalizing is when we take one example as the rule for all possible occurrences. Cultural stereotypes are often in this form: Americans can't speak foreign languages, All Italians eat spaghetti, All men are ..., All women are ... Other key words to let you know you are over-generalizing are *always, never, only, everybody, nobody.*

Catastrophizing is negatively **exaggerating**, or what Borysenko (1987) calls awfulizing, making a mountain out of a molehill (something big from something really insignificant). When some people are late, they may start thinking of all kinds of negative thoughts, like, "If I'm late they're going to think that I don't care and they won't like me and I'll never make any friends and everyone will hate me. This always happens to me!" As you can see, catastrophizers find over-generalization very useful. They also cop out and demand a lot.

Copping out is when we blame others or circumstances instead of taking responsibility ourselves: "I was late because my mother didn't wake me up early enough," or, "I can't learn because he is a bad teacher," or, "He always makes me unhappy." Of course some things are the fault of others, but in general we can decide what we think of them – and we can achieve much more when we take responsibility for as much as we can. Then we can exercise more control over ourselves and the situation, and get more done. Key words to notice are: *because, fault, makes me,* etc.

Lastly, **demanding** is something that MUST be done. We tell ourselves that we have to, **have got to**, or must do something. For example, "I've got to pass this next test," or "I've got to clean my room today," or "I must get up early tomorrow." Changing these to "I would like to ..." or "I have decided to ..." are closer to reality, take some of the stress off you, allow you to see alternatives and enable you to feel more in control of your own life.

Demanding that things and other people should be different can also cause a lot of frustration. Insisting "It must be sunny tomorrow or else!" or "They should change!" creates our own frustration. It's nice to keep in mind the wisdom of the serenity prayer:

The four junkthoughts are irrational beliefs. When they occur automatically in our thinking, they can cause problems and negative feelings. Recognizing them in ourselves and others helps us to monitor what is going on in our brains – and then we can **challenge them** when it is helpful to do so.

Recognizing junkthoughts

When we are learning a foreign language, it's a good time to examine the kind of language we already have in our minds and think about what kind of language we want to put in.

Task 1: Look at the underlined words in the first paragraph below and see if you can name what kinds of junkthought they are. Then try the second paragraph.

a) "Of course everybody must know about these four junkthoughts or they will end up thinking terrible things and become extremely stressed and their lives will become total failures. And it will all be our parents' fault because they didn't explain to us how we have to think."

b) "He always spoils my day with the way he looks at me. He should learn how to smile more, then we could all do good work. Until then we'll never do the work we must do to succeed. The company will probably go bankrupt in the end."

Also notice the way this kind of language makes you feel.

Task 2: Find a friend and have some fun. Each person tells the other some junkthought that they hear (or use) occasionally, and the other says what kind of junkthought it is.

Task 3: Write a passage of junkthought that you might use habitually in some area of your life, and make it worse than you normally do. Exaggerate it and have fun with it. Then notice how you catch yourself the next time it happens. And notice how you can laugh at it and change it!

Challenging junkthoughts

Often the easiest way to challenge a junkthought that you hear from yourself or others is simply to repeat it in a questioning way, or to exaggerate it even more. For example:

Over-generalizing: "It always rains when ..." or, "Everyone's in a bad mood today."
Challenge: (repeat the key word) "Always?" "Everyone?"

Catastrophizing: "I'll die if I fail this test!"
Challenge: (exaggerate, with a touch of humour) "Really? Can I have your lunch if you die?"

Copping Out: "I was late because I had a phone call at the last minute."
Challenge: (again, exaggerate with a touch of humour): "You poor thing, people do cause you problems. You're right – there's absolutely nothing you can do."

Demanding: "I must ...", "I have to ..."
Challenge: (draw attention to other options) "What will happen if you don't?"

Warning: Be careful when you use these challenges. Using them with people who don't know about this information can damage relationships. People may not like their thinking being challenged.
One student I know became so enthusiastic about challenging junkthought that she almost lost her boyfriend. When I met them, he said, "She's always repeating what I say; that really makes me angry." She couldn't help interrupting him just then and saying, "Always?"

Sometimes these patterns may be unconscious internal dialogue, self-talk, and you hardly notice them. But once you realize you may have a pattern, then you can change it by simply challenging it in a fun and loving way.

We are what we are because we have been doing the best we can with what we've got. So we can be kind to ourselves, and simply change for the better.

When we go to work or school, we go the best way we know. When we find a shorter or better way, we change our habits quickly, and we understand that before we had been doing the best we could – we just hadn't known better.

We can change our thinking habits in the same way. Whatever we think now is okay.

But it can get better. And for those who want it, that's an interesting adventure for the mind.

For a very readable introduction to mind-body healing get: Borysenko, J. 1987, *Minding the Body, Mending the Mind.* New York: Bantam Books.
Concerning junkthought, an easy read is *Thinking, Changing, Rearranging* by Jill Anderson, Portland, Oregon: Meta-morphous Press, 1981 **or in Japanese** by Masayasu Itou, 1990, published by Kodansha.

CHAPTER 14
Focusing on Attention: Where is Your Seven, Plus or Minus Two?

CHAPTER 14
Focusing on Attention: Where is Your Seven, Plus or Minus Two?

"Whatever touches the heart is engraved in memory."
Voltaire

Think about it first!
1. How many things can you think about at the same time?
2. How can you focus more on one thing at a time?
3. How can you remember more of what you hear in conversations and lectures?

The chances are that you've got a lot on your mind at any one time. Your work, a faraway friend, some special place, a hobby, something to eat, an important project … You may see pictures. You may hear voices or sounds. You may also have feelings that are sparked by thinking about someone special or an activity that you love doing.

Seven, plus or minus two

In 1956 the psychologist George Miller wrote an article about our short-term memories. He found that most of us have the capacity to remember 7 ± 2 – which means from five to nine – pieces of unrelated information. These may be numbers (as in seven-digit telephone numbers), words, or anything else.

When these unrelated things come in meaningful chunks with relationships, they are easier to remember. Take, for example: 23 45 67. If you know a good friend who is 23 and who has a big nose that makes a 45-degree angle and he lives on 67th street, you have given meaning to the chunks that will help you remember. You could take a minute to memorize these numbers in this way – or you could re-chunk them and make them even easier to remember. See how easy it would be if you pushed them all together and made one long number. (Try it now!)

Out to lunch?

Language learning depends partly upon our short-term memory being able to seize upon what we hear for a long enough time to attach some sort of meaning to it. The 7 ± 2 could also be called our **attention capacity**. If, during a class, half of our attention is focused on last weekend, the tennis court, or a special person, then we won't be able to handle much new information. That this happens quite often is revealed in how often we hear people say, "I just couldn't focus on the class" or, "I was thinking about other things." In slang English we sometimes jokingly say, "He's here, but his mind's out to lunch!"

Self Regulatory Speech

Often, when we need to focus our attention – for example, when we're adding a list of numbers – we talk to ourselves out loud. And if, when one person is doing that, another person teases them by saying a few random numbers out loud, the counter may have to stop, and then start over again, because the 7 ± 2 that they needed to complete the task has been disrupted.

I can still hear my mother talking to herself as she was getting dinner ready for a family of seven. I often see tennis players on TV talking to themselves between points. Young children who have just acquired speech also talk to themselves while doing activities. When you take a test, you may talk a lot to yourself as you try to figure out the right answer. Psychologists call this self-regulatory speech, and it allows you to use language to direct action, to focus all your 7 ± 2 on the task.

What happens in a typical classroom is very different. You know you can look straight at a teacher, even smile and nod, and in your mind still be singing karaoke last Saturday night. Your body is there, but your mind is out to lunch. But what if you really do want to concentrate on what is happening and you want to give your 7 ± 2 to what is going on? What if you could give all your attention to learning, and enjoy it?

Getting excited!

There are several ways to focus your attention. The most crucial element is your decision to really want to learn. Our minds naturally think about things that we feel are important to us.

When we make the decision that learning language is important to us, then focusing comes naturally. When we **get excited about learning**, we look for opportunities to learn more. If the topic is not interesting or if we are distracted by other things, outside or inside our brains, then we naturally give our attention to those things.

So getting motivated and excited are important. *Setting goals for our learning usually helps us get excited.* Also finding fun ways to learn will encourage our natural attention.

Shadowing

In Chapter 4, I wrote about shadowing, which is repeating what one hears, either out loud or silently in one's mind. The positive and encouraging feedback from students tells me that this simple technique has great potential and that we should try it more.

When you repeat what you hear, it gets you to focus more attention on it and it keeps stray thoughts away. You don't need to wait to be highly focused in order for self-regulatory speech to start. Instead, you can get yourself highly focused by shadowing whoever is speaking.

My students tell me that shadowing helps them to understand lectures in their native language as well as in languages they are learning. Some students become automatic repeating machines of whatever they decide they want to learn, whether in lectures, on cassettes, video and TV, or in conversations. They have become childlike imitators of their environment, with their 7 ± 2 focused outwardly.

WHERE IS YOUR 7 ± 2 ?

You see, when we are children we imitate and repeat (shadow and echo) whatever is presented to us. Our brains do this naturally. Then, as we grow, we develop self-talk, and begin giving our brains our own input; teenagers probably deal with as much self-input as they do with information from their surroundings. Adult brains may have even more self-talk, which can be hard to stop.

This may be one reason that children seem to learn so fast; their sensory receptors are focused externally, and they are intensively involved in mapping what they hear and see. Adults, who have already largely mapped their environment, tend to take in new information in small bits, and hook it onto old information that is similar. So they often don't look at the new closely enough to see how it is different; they look mostly at what is already in their minds.

Adults also talk to themselves a lot. This can be useful sometimes, but some-times it can get in the way. If our own self-talk is very loud, then we don't hear much of what is being said to us by others. Shadowing allows us to become childlike again, and to focus more of our attention externally, to calm our internal commentary.

Conversational Shadowing

My students report that shadowing a lecture or film, while useful, is tiring, especially when the material is not easy to understand. When you shadow a lecture or film, the speakers never hear your shadowing and don't have the chance to adjust to your level of comprehension. Much of what they say may be too difficult, but they don't know this, so they just keep talking.

At these times, shadowing may not be easy. My students say they can usually shadow lectures in foreign languages only in short spurts of around 10—20 minutes. So maybe teachers should not talk for more than 10 minutes, and then let students summarize.

Conversational shadowing, on the other hand, is done out loud with a single partner, and is basically reflective. When a shadower cannot repeat what a speaker says, the speaker adjusts to the listener's level. And if you do conversational shadowing with a native speaker, it gets them to chunk language and information, to offer simple explanations, and in general to create a better relationship

through reflective listening (although there may be moments of frustration until the NS learns how to adjust).

When you shadow in a conversation, you might choose to shadow only parts of it (echoing) and to make some grammatical transformations. For example, when your partner says, "I went to the store," you would transform it to, "You went to the store."

The speaker can tell right away if they need to repeat parts or to explain further because the listener may repeat only a part, perhaps leaving another part unsaid, or repeat something other than what the speaker actually said, or repeat it word for word, but with rising intonation that signals a question as to the meaning. All these adjustments are made naturally in our everyday conversation, and we don't have to think about them; we only have to remember to shadow.

Remembering to shadow, and summarizing

With shadowing, the speaker can tell right away if they need to repeat parts or to explain further. The listener has many options: repeat word for word, repeat only a part, repeat with rising intonation to question, change the words to your own, give "please continue" signals, or any mix of these. Some ask me to write it in the corner of the blackboard as a reminder. Others write an S on their hand or turn their watches upside down as reminders. Still others write the word SHADOW on their textbooks and on their cassettes for the language lab. I've found I can help them to do it more, in both lectures and conversation, when I begin talking and then shadow my own speech out loud for a few lines. This turns their brains on! And then I stop and ask them to summarize with a partner.

The Din

After you have shadowed and summarized for a short length of time, you often get a bonus gift that follows you around: the Din. A din is a continuous hum, like the sound a computer or air-conditioner might make. After being in contact with a foreign language for a while and then having an interval of quiet, learners often notice that the language starts flowing back through the brain like a din, with no conscious effort. Shadowing seems to make this happen even more. This is our mind working overtime on learning, and it indicates when acquisition of language is deepening.

Incorporation: language as part of you

Finally, shadowing allows you to be one with the language. You are what you hear, because you say it yourself as well. Neurologist Oliver Sachs, author of *Awakenings,* explains it this way:

The "other side" of body-image losses are all the incorporations into body-image of one's skis or one's scalpels - or, for that matter, the car or plane one pilots. Nothing feels "natural", "comes naturally" until it is incorporated ... In learning sports (or, for that matter, ballet-dancing, or pancake tossing) one has, I think, to start with a "mimesis"; no abstract description or explication can be incorporated as part of self. I suppose something of the sort is operative in language acquisition (personal communication).

WHAT'S ON YOUR MIND?

Miller, G. A., 1956. 'The magical number seven, plus or minus two: Some limits on our capacity for processing information.' *Psychological Review* 63:81—97.

CHAPTER 15
Passion, Vision and Action

CHAPTER 15
Passion, Vision and Action

"Keep away from people who try to belittle your ambitions. Small people do that, but the really great make you feel that you, too, can become great."

Mark Twain

Think about it first!
1. How do Olympians think differently from most of us?
2. Can we learn how to use our minds as they use their minds?

As a teenager, Olympian Marilyn King was an average student who enjoyed sports. At the Eastern States High School Championships one year, they announced that they only had two participants for the pentathlon and they needed a third in order to hold the event. The pentathlon has five events – hurdles, shot-put, high jump, long jump and the 200-metre sprint. Marilyn volunteered, and was happy to come third.

She decided to train a bit; the next year she came first, and was sent to the national pentathlon championships in California. There she was placed in the top ten in the nation. Then something happened that changed her life. The Olympic committee was there to select athletes to work with. They chose two girls Marilyn had beaten. One was a fine athlete who had just performed badly on the day of the competition. However, Marilyn knew she was better than the other athlete who'd been selected.

Of course, Marilyn was disappointed. But then she reasoned: "If they chose her, and I beat her, that means that I could go to the Olympics. **I could go to the Olympics!**" This last phrase ran through her head over and over again when she returned home.

She said it as she ran around the track, and she imagined actually walking one day into the Olympic stadium on opening day. Suddenly training became easier, and she found herself more motivated. Whenever she said, "I could go to the Olympics," the things that she needed to do in order to actually get there would pop into her head.

Marilyn was not really much different from other teenagers her age. When the alarm clock went off at five in the morning for her workout, she had a tendency to think, "Oh, I'm too tired, I'll sleep a few more hours, and train twice as much tonight." But as she lay there, the image of herself walking into the Olympic stadium would pop into her head, and she would smile, and get excited. And she just couldn't stay in bed – she would get up and run!

Marilyn says now that most people think that Olympic athletes have a lot of *will-power* and *determination*, and that's what enables them to work so hard. But she says no, it's not that – it's the vision. It's the power of an image that inspires great passion and excitement – so much so that you have enormous energy to do what you want. That's what others may call determination and will-power. However, for her it was the excitement of a vision that inspired great passion to act.

Marilyn realized her dream and went to two Olympics. She decided to try one more time and this time to really channel all her energies into it. She took a year off to devote her time to training, something she had never done before. Then, nine months before the national trials for the Olympics, she was in a terrible car accident and seriously injured her back. For four months she had to lie on her couch in extreme pain, unable even to change position.

Then she started looking at a few video tapes of the superstars in each of her five events. She found they distracted her from the pain and that she felt better looking at them. She imagined in her mind that the person on the screen was really *her* doing all these events, and she would send little messages to her muscles telling them what they should be doing. She obtained more video tapes, and watched them over and over again. Later, she went out to the track and watched other people doing the events. She imagined they were her. Gradually she started moving and walking again. And then, slowly, to jog. Amazingly, at the trials for her third Olympics, with very little training, she qualified second.

Marilyn realized after her miraculous recovery that something important had happened in her mind: that her body had reacted to her image training, and that this process could be used for more important things than just running around a track. She started bringing together other ex-Olympians to find out if they had had similar experiences.

She discovered that most Olympians had a very clear vision of what they wanted, and that this vision was strongly present in their minds. The vision (or goal or outcome) also inspired great passion and excitement. The vision and the passion inspired them to take a lot of action, over and over again. To do something about it.

Dreamers, Workaholics, and Bound to the Ground

We all seem to have different quantities of Passion, Vision, and Action in different contexts. For example, occasionally we have a Vision of being a film star, and it's exciting. However, most of us never take any Action in this direction; we only dream. Either the Vision is not clear enough or repetitive enough, or the Passion is not strong enough. For most of us, it's simply a nice daydream.

Sometimes we have a great Passion and we do a great amount of work (Action) – but we don't accomplish much because we don't have a clear Vision. Without the Vision, without choosing a specific goal, we may work on a lot of things that go in a lot of different directions. When we do this we might call ourselves workaholics.

Sometimes we do have some vague Vision and we actually do take some Actions – but for some reason we don't get excited about the vision and thus don't take a lot of action. It's the Passion that's missing. For example, many people get an education, but they never learn to become passionate about it.

Getting Them All Together and BIG

When our goals are too vague, we don't get excited about them. Watching King Kong on a small black and white TV is not

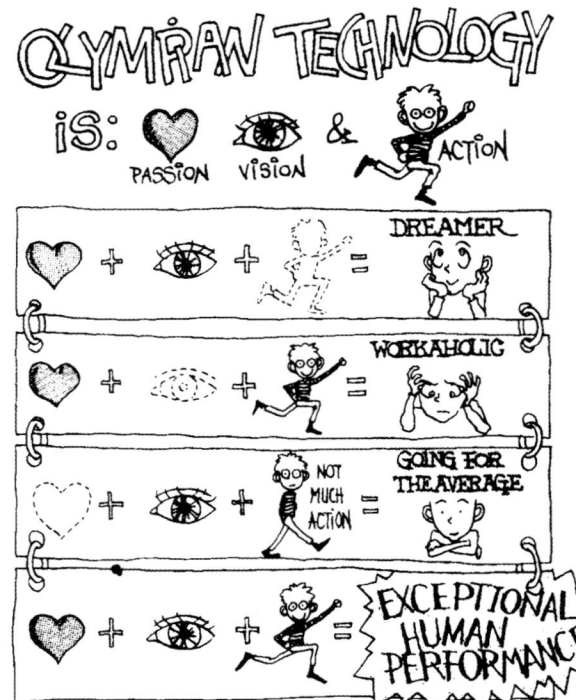

CHAPTER 15: Passion, Vision and Action

very frightening. But when you go to a cinema with quadraphonic sound, a 30-metre screen and a friend who grabs your arm when things really get scary, King Kong is impressive. When you leave the cinema, you begin looking over the tops of buildings to see if you see any hairy heads popping up. So why not help yourself, and do this with your goals?

The most important thing is to select goals and make them specific. That's what successful Olympians, artists, business people and scientists do. Their visions are so impressive that their body and mind react and are training all the time.

Play with your brain

Take, for example, one of your own minor goals. Stop, now, and think of one … Think about it and notice what kind of feelings it might inspire in you. If you don't get excited about it, then you probably won't get around to doing much about it. And if you do, you probably won't give it a lot of time or passion.

Now take that goal and make an imaginary picture of it just a few feet away from your face. Then let the picture grow very quickly in size until it's a 30-metre-square film screen. Go ahead, do it! This chapter can wait …

Welcome back. How was it? Most people notice an amazing shift in their feelings toward the once minor goal – they may even become passionate about it. Basically, it's become more appealing.

After you think about what has happened, you may decide you don't want to get super-excited about that one minor goal and spend too much time on it. You may want to pick a really important goal … like, for example, language learning.

With this more important goal, in addition to putting it onto a big screen, you may add colour, sound, and motion. You might experiment with even bringing it closer, or jumping into it as if into virtual reality. Each person's brain may react differently

to these different changes. It's up to you to play with your own brain and find out what makes your images most attractive to you, what makes you want to really accomplish the things you imagine.

Actions to Take

Marilyn King found out, when she talked with other Olympians, that once the Vision got big and the Passion grew, the Actions that she needed to take just suddenly presented themselves; they popped up as if by magic. For example, she realized in high school that to be an Olympian she would have to change her diet and find a good coach.

Actually, I feel the signposts to accomplish your dreams are already posted and waiting for you. When you *specify your dreams* then you start to *see the signposts*. When you want to drive to a certain town, your vision becomes 'sticky' for the signs that will lead you there, and you ignore irrelevant signs. But if you don't know where you want to go, all signs have equal value, and choosing what to look at is difficult. Your vision, the image of your goal, makes you sensitive to those things that will lead you there. And then it becomes easier to choose the right actions to take.

And if you make your goals specific, this can make them easier to visualize and easier to attain. We'll talk about such **well-formed outcomes** in the next chapter. In the meantime, Dare to Imagine!

---

* I met Marilyn King in June 1994 at a conference in Finland. We even went jogging together (because we were late catching a boat). So now I can say I trained with an Olympic athlete. While she makes big money talking to corporations, she works with inner-city kids getting them to Dare to Imagine goals and a better life. She also works with Olympic athletes worldwide who are promoting peace and getting people to Dare to Imagine. I am using her book *Dare to Imagine*

(which is for high school students in the US), with my first-year university students. Her company address is Beyond Sports, 484—149 Lake Park Avenue, Oakland, CA 94610, USA.

CHAPTER 15
Your Specific Successes and
New Year's Resolutions

CHAPTER 16
Your Specific Successes and New Year's Resolutions

*"Every human being has the freedom
to change at any instant."*
Viktor Frankl

Think about it first!
1. How can you create goals that you can really succeed at?
2. What characteristics of goals make them easier to achieve?

The chances are that the two expressions in the title, *Specific successes* and *New Year's resolutions*, create different reactions in most readers. And my guess is that while you are drawn to the second and the fun of dreaming of making resolutions, you probably can't remember the ones from past years and what happened to them after making them. They were vague clouds that drifted off to Who-knows-where-land.

But your specific successes. Now that calls up some real pictures in your mind – times and places when you succeeded! And the chances are that you know just how much you succeeded and in what ways. They are pleasant memories.

Could the two be connected? Could your resolutions turn into your specific successes? If so, how would it happen? My guess is that most resolutions, and many of the goals we create all year long, fall by the wayside because they don't have the quality of an *achievable outcome* in the first place. They don't meet the criteria of a well-formed outcome. So this is my Christmas present to you. When you've got these criteria satisfied, your outcomes will be more possible, and achieving them becomes more fun. And overcoming the obstacles becomes even more interesting.

In the last chapter, I described Marilyn King's ideas of Olympian thinking: basically, when you have a clear Vision and great Passion, you take lots of appropriate Actions which produce high performance. The following criteria are a refinement of this.

Before going on, take a minute now to write a list of your goals – a few short-term and a few long-term ones. Go ahead; take a minute to write some down. Or, if you can find it, use your list of New Year's resolutions.

Now, as you read on through this article, you can apply the criteria to your own real goals.

PC SERSEF

The mnemonic for remembering these criteria is PC SERSEF. I think of my PC (personal computer) doing a special serve self search that will come up with some great results. Also, the strangeness of SERSEF makes it easy to remember.

P stands for **Positive**. It is well known that your brain's way of imagining a negative is first to actually create the concept and then try to cross it out. When you read, "Don't think of an elephant", you first think of an elephant and then maybe try to put an X through it. Sometimes this is a great way to get someone to actually think of something, although you are telling them not to; Mary Poppins sings "Don't close your eyes" to get children to go to sleep.

So whatever your goal is, formulate it with a positive image in mind. Not 'I don't want to smoke any more' but 'I want to breathe easily' or 'I want to smell nice' or 'I want to be healthy'. Not 'I don't want to be shy' but 'I want to be outgoing'.

C stands for **Control**, your control. Is the power to accomplish this goal within your control? Basically you can control just about anything having to do with yourself. But other people and things are often not under your control. For example, 'I want to make that person love me' is not a goal under your control. But 'I am going to make myself a lovable person' is under your control, and will probably serve you better in the long run anyway.

S stands for **Sensory Specific**. Make your goals as specific as possible – then your brain sees a clearer image, hears what others will say, and has a particular feeling that is very motivating. Then your excited brain will find things to do to accomplish your goal. 'I want to improve my speaking' is too vague and it doesn't usually move people. Something specific like, 'I want to get 500 on TOEFL' or 'I want to pass the fourth level of the test next spring and hear myself speaking on the telephone' are things that are more precise and will motivate you to do something. (This is why test-taking is so popular – you get specific results – and at times devastating!) Furthermore, you can state the time frame: for example, 'in the next six months', and it will move you more. When you make goals specific, then mid-term goals become evident: for example, you can calculate how many words you have to learn per month.

E stands for **Evidence**. As you work toward your goal, what evidence will you have that you are getting closer? In studying for a specific test, you may count the number of vocabulary items that you've already learned. In becoming healthier, you might measure how much stronger, faster, or more flexible you are becoming. You might notice how good you feel about it. This evidence is good to know about

beforehand, because then you will recognize these things more easily when they happen. If you don't think about them beforehand, you may not recognize them, and you may think you are not progressing and then not want to continue.

R stands for **Resources**. Do you have, or can you find, the resources you need to accomplish your goal? Listing the resources you have and the resources you need will help you to see how you will accomplish your goal. The resources may be books and materials, which you can buy (or borrow from friends or a library). People are resources. You also have a lot of resources right inside of you: your perseverance, your curiosity, your ability to …

The second **S** is for **Size**. If your goal is too small, it may not excite you enough for you to really pursue it. If it is too big, it may seem impossible and you won't start. This also depends on the person. Some people are really motivated by a big dream and it moves them to take massive action. However, even they can be helped by having intermediate-size mid-term goals that they can accomplish on the way to the big goal. Other people prefer to look at the mid-term goal only, and if that goes okay, then they will look at and dream of the next step. What motivates you? What gets you to move? Think big and exciting, and also think of what the mid-term goals are, those important progress markers.

E stands for **Ecology**. Imagine what happens if you really do succeed in your goal and get it. Will it cause any problems in other areas? For example, becoming thin may mean you won't have enough energy for sports you enjoy. Is it still worth it to you? Stopping smoking may not be a good idea if it makes you fat and grouchy all the time. So you need to figure out ecological ways to stop smoking without other bad consequences before this becomes an ecological outcome.

One way to check the ecology is to think 'as if' you have already succeeded. Then just notice how you are and what other things change. If there are problems, you can sometimes change part of the goal, or how you go about it, to solve these problems beforehand, so that they won't occur. Sometimes you may decide that the goal is not as important as preserving balance in the other systems. If you really want to make a million dollars, you might have to sacrifice something.

F stands for **First Step**. What is your first step to succeeding in your goal? What can you do right now, today, that will start you on the way? *A journey of a thousand miles starts with a single step.* And that first step starts from where you are. It can be as simple as going to the library, making an appointment or writing a plan. A first step might be to make a list of things that you can already do now. Then – do those things! Get started! Make a plan, and put it on your door.

Notice that actually doing something towards achieving your goal confirms it and motivates you to take more action. Identifying your first steps gives you momentum – it gets the ball rolling. Nothing succeeds like success, so plan on being successful in a small way already, now, at the beginning.

P   positive
C   control
S   sensory specific
E   evidence
R   resources
S   size
E   ecology
F   first steps

Finally, after you have well-formed outcomes, you may want to take a moment to inspire yourself by intensifying them.

1) Make a really rich and wonderful **VISION** of your goal in as much detail as possible. Make the picture big and colourful, with stereo sound.

2) Then you might decide to allow this vision to create intensely powerful **PASSION** in you.

3) With this **VISION** and **PASSION** you will probably see the **ACTIONS** that you want to take to get there.

Then, just DO IT! Remember that while we do, most of the fun is in getting there, and in getting over the obstacles as they make us jump higher and farther. Enjoy the road!

Smart Fun!
Know your goals
Write them down:
1. Three major goals for this week
2. Three major goals for this year
3. Three major goals for the next four years
4. Three major goals for your life
5. Check all your goals with PCSERSEF
6. Think of three people who are role models for you, and describe the characteristics that you admire about them
7. What is the common thread between your goals and the people you esteem? This is your *mission* in life
8. What can you do today that will contribute toward your major life goals?

CHAPTER 17
Collaboration: When Students
Learn Most from Each Other

CHAPTER 17
Collaboration: When Students Learn Most from Each Other

"Some thoughts from David Mayer, edited and added to."
by Tim Murphey

Think about it first!
1. What are the effects of thinking you are shy?
2. Do you think you are a shy person?
3. What are the effects of thinking that everyone else is better?

Father David Mayer is a white-haired, soft-spoken, easy-smiling professor of literature. He gets on well with his students. He believes in them and wants them to become all they can be. He has found three ideas that sometimes stop them from learning. These ideas are **false beliefs** that can be easily changed when you understand them.

He tells his students about these ideas at the beginning of each year. Understanding them allows students to relax and learn more. They are:
1. I'm shy.
2. Everybody else is better.
3. I'm not good enough any more.

1. Shy?
Mayer explains that students often say, "I'm shy." Of course some people may really be shy. But most of us are not shy with our classmates. In fact we make a lot of noise when we speak with each other.

There is the normal human tendency to dislike being a fool in public. When we have to perform in a foreign language we sometimes feel foolish, and we fear making mistakes. When you understand that it is natural to make mistakes, you stop using the excuse 'I'm shy' and start to be more active in starting conversations and asking questions. But when you realize that making mistakes is okay, you can take risks. Then you really learn a lot because you can talk more joyfully with your classmates and friends in your target language.

2. Everybody else is better; 'The grass is always greener on the other side'.
The thought that others are better can, along with a sense of perfectionism, discourage students. In language learning, it is natural that some learners know words or patterns that others don't. This is not something for you to worry about, but to be happy about, because you can learn these new words and constructions directly from classmates without having to look them up in dictionaries and grammar books. Also, what should be important to you is not how much others know, but how much you have learned and been able to use through participation in the class.

Two mottoes are important here: 'Pool your knowledge and learn from each other', and 'Never compare yourself with others; compare yourself only with yourself'. You need to think about your own progress. If you can speak more or understand a little more of a conversation than you did two weeks or a month ago, then you are doing fine. No matter what the others are doing, you are making progress. The class is not a sports event where you are out to win a gold medal. Your aim instead is to progress in using English for communication. Students have often said later that the saying 'Never compare yourself with others; compare yourself only with yourself' gave them the biggest boost in their English studies that year.

3. I'm not Top Dog any more

Because in many countries it has become possible to analyze the levels of universities and junior colleges, students at more or less the same level enter the same departments in college. Whereas they might have been at the top of their class in their high school, when they get to university they find that they are only one of many people who are evenly matched.

If you're one of these, not only do you have to try more and be more daring to learn more to keep up with the others, but you also need to keep a positive attitude when you find things difficult. You need to stay encouraged. You are not less smart; it is only that you are now among equals.

But because you are all so talented, you can share your knowledge and become even better. The sooner you trust each other, the quicker you will create an atmosphere in which you can dare to speak your target language and be accepted by the group. With trust, you can all learn something from each other and feel free to make progress.

(Original version published in *The Language Teacher*, May 1994)

A fourth misconception held by students is: 'I can only learn from the teacher'. But much research shows that students actually learn a lot from each other when they dare to interact in the target language (see Chapter 2).

Collaborative learning, cooperative learning, peer tutoring and research on near-peer role models all point to the fact that the people sitting beside you in your classes can teach you a lot, and you can learn a lot by teaching them. It's also more relaxing and more fun to learn from your friends and classmates.

Ask each other regularly: 'What are you learning?' and teach others what you are learning. It makes learning much more pleasurable.

FIND A FRIEND TO COLLABORATE WITH AND MAKE LEARNING **FUN**!

CHAPTER 18
From Learned Helplessness
to SPURR

CHAPTER 18
From Learned Helplessness to SPURR

"Use it or lose it! "
Anon

Think about it first!
1. What are the differences between the ways that A-grade and C-grade students study?
2. Are the ways that you study effective?

Learned helplessness

I often tell my students about an experiment that was done with rats. Rats are really quite intelligent, and are usually very resourceful when it comes to avoiding pain and finding food.

In the experiment, a rat was put in a cage and given irregular, small electric shocks through the floor of the cage. The rat jumped around and tried to find a way out. But there was none, and the rat found this out after four or five minutes. It then just sat on the floor, took the shocks and whined.

Then came the really interesting part of the experiment. The same rat was put in a different cage, which had a lever that the rat could push to stop the shocks. Rats regularly learn to press such levers to get rewards. However, this rat, having learned in the previous cage that there was no way out, over-generalized, and in the new cage just sat and took the electric shocks. It had learned to be helpless – thus the term 'learned helplessness'.

I tell my students that people often act in the same way. We do the best we can in difficult situations. Then, when we feel that we have no control, we may give up trying new things. Even when shown better ways to learn, many people insist that they already know how to learn and have been doing it all their lives.

Students often don't try new ways which might be more effective, make life more enjoyable and study time more efficient. By the time we get to university, we all have been conditioned by 12 years of schooling. That's a lot of time spent in forming habits.

I invite you to Dare to Imagine for a moment that the way you learned in school might have been a type of learned helplessness. Now you could become more active and experiment with different ways to learn and think. It is not only my students, but all of us, including me, who are in danger of being too comfortable with our limiting beliefs and strategies. So we don't experiment with new ways to learn and live.

But it can be fun, for a change, to look for better ways and to experiment with different ways of using our brain.

Learner strategies of effective students

In 1981, Mary-Ann Reiss asked several groups of language students to describe what they would do to complete three assignments, and then to answer a general question. How would you respond to them? Think about them for yourself and jot down the activities you would do.

1. Learn a list of 30 vocabulary items taken from a reading selection which you have recently completed.

2. Learn a new [verb] tense. The tense has been explained in class. You are given a list of regular verbs.

3. Answer a series of questions after a reading selection. This selection has not been read in class.

4. What strategies or techniques have helped you most when studying a foreign language? What strategy, if any, do you use when studying a foreign language which you might not use when studying another subject?

Reiss then asked her students to write down on their papers the grades, A, B, C or D, that they had achieved in their courses the year before. She then sorted the papers by grade. She set the B-grade to one side, and put the A-grade student strategies side by side with the C-grade and D-grade. She wanted to see a contrast between what the 'effective' A-grade students were doing and the 'ineffective' C-grade and D-grade students. She listed the features, and I've included her list at the end of this chapter.

I've used this list for a number of years to alert my students to their own ways of studying and to open up their minds to possible alternative ways to study. Before reading on, you may want to look through the list yourself and mark which ones you use.

Most students find that they have been using a lot of C/D-grade strategies for most of their schooling; exam-driven school systems usually direct students to use them. So if you have been depending on them, you could learn more material faster by trying some A-grade strategies.

Differences between A-grade and C/D-grade strategies: SPURR.

Look at the list again, and take a moment to find the general differences between the A-grade group and the C/D-grade group. List these on a sheet of paper.

A-grade students typically come up with what I call SPURR: Specifically Personal Use Repeated and Recycled.

The A-grade student strategies are usually **Specific** and multi-sensory. In other words, we can see exactly what they are doing – 'I talk to myself while I jog' – while the C/D strategies are vague and we aren't really sure how they do what they do – 'I study, repeat, memorize ...'

A-grade students also use new language in **Personal** ways to remember it better. They think of people they know and things they do, and then relate them to the new words.

They find situations in their daily life when they can **Use** these words. These students seem to incorporate language into their very being; they make it part of themselves. But C/D-grade students study language as an object outside of themselves. It's not part of them, something to use in their everyday life. A-grade students use what they are learning, C/D-grade students only study it.

Finally, both A-grade and C/D-grade students **Repeat** and **Recycle**. However, the C/D-grade students repeat what they are learning in impersonal, boring ways, as though studying for a test, and make it hard work. But A-grade students repeat and recycle in fun, personal interactions with other people in many situations. They actually *use* the new things they are learning.

Moreover, A-grade students seem to realize that they can learn anywhere, at any time, with anyone, and they use downtime creatively. (Downtime is time you usually think is wasted, like waiting for a bus.) A-grade students take the opportunity of downtime to talk to themselves or review some expressions they want to memorize.

JUST DO IT!

Look in your notebooks and find some expressions and vocabulary to SPURR. Think of specifically personal ways to use the things you want to learn in your regular everyday life. While this takes a bit of time initially, you will find that you will remember the material longer and that it is more fun to learn things when you are really using them. And after a while, the strategy becomes natural and you just do it all the time.

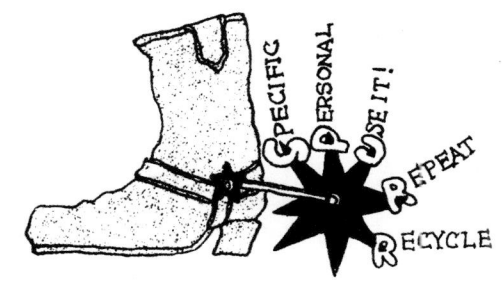

What would you do to complete these assignments?

ANSWERS FROM A–GRADE STUDENTS	ANSWERS FROM C/D–GRADE STUDENTS

1) **Your assignment is to learn a list of 30 vocabulary items taken from a reading selection which you have recently completed.**

- Make up a sentence with each word	- Memorize
- Put cue (hint) next to each word on list	- Write out and memorize
- Say words out loud while memorizing	- Put on index cards
- Tape words and listen to cassette	- Study until learned
- Sing words out loud	- Write out and memorize
- Write word on one side of paper, definition or synonym on other	- Repeat many times mentally
- Use new words as much as possible	- Write and memorize
	- List according to parts of speech

2) **Your assignment is to learn a new [verb] tense. The tense has been explained in class. You are given a list of regular verbs.**

- Look over reading and try to find examples of new tense	- Study until understood
- Try to practise new tense while speaking	- Go over rules and memorize
- Write, say, and use it in examples	- Repeat and write out
- Look for similar endings already known	- Keep going over it
- Make up own exercise to practise new tense	- Repeat many times
- Learn and make up examples (sentences)	- Try to understand the English counterpart
	- Go over rules and class notes

3) Your assignment is to answer a series of questions after a reading selection. This selection has not been read in class.

- First answer easy questions, then reread and answer the rest
- Skim the reading and look up answers
- Look for "key" word in questions and find them in answers
- Look for words in questions which give clues to answers
- Answer each question mentally, then write out
- Answer as much as possible, then re-read selection for remaining questions

- Read questions, use dictionary to look up words
- Translate selection, translate questions
- Translate questions and flip back to reading
- Use dictionary and grammar book
- Keep going back to selection for answers
- Look up all unfamiliar words, then answer questions

4) What strategies or techniques have helped you most when studying a foreign language? What strategy, if any, do you use when studying a foreign language which you might not use when studying another subject?

- I speak to myself while walking or jogging
- I use association (mental pictures)
- I give myself little tests
- I write down key points of each chapter
- I speak to my friends or natives when I get the chance
- I make lists and study sheets, and try to remember by rhyming and association
- I try to answer all questions mentally in class
- I use mnemonic devices to remember [1 = pen, 2 = swan, or 1 = bun, 2 = shoe]

- I study with someone
- I jot information on index cards
- I write new information over and over
- I use the Appendix in book (things in the back)
- I remember by association and repetition
- I look over my notes regularly
- I translate everything into (my native language)
- I make up lists and read them out loud

CHAPTER 19
Getting Pleasantly Soaked:
Input and Output Flooding

CHAPTER 19
Getting Pleasantly Soaked: Input and Output Flooding

"If you always do what you have always done, you will always get what you have always got" Anon *"Embrace adventure and dance with the unknown"* Tanak Akay

Think about it first!
1. What ways do you have of repeatedly seeing or hearing the things you want to learn?
2. What ways can you exercise using the language you are learning?

It's a common experience that the words we hear most often seem to be the easiest to learn. And the words we use most often are the ones we really learn. For example, it's difficult for foreigners in any country not to learn 'please' and 'thank you', because these expressions seem to occur at least 10 times in nearly every encounter.

However, words that are not repeated quite so often seem a bit more difficult to learn. Wouldn't it be nice if the words we really wanted to learn were often spoken in our environment ? "Yes," I hear you say, "but they just aren't." You're right. They are not in your environment enough – unless you **do your own environmental engineering**.

In Chapter 10, I suggested recording things you wanted to learn and then playing the tape to yourself often. This would remind you of the words and help you think about using them. This is an example of what researchers are calling **Input Flooding**. And there are many more ways to do it.

When we observe a small child interacting with Mum and Dad, we find that the parents have a pretty good idea which words the child already knows. They repeat these words a lot, and they repeat new words even more often. But older students don't usually have parents who do this. And other adults won't usually repeat as much with you as they do with a child. So it's up to you to find ways to get the repetitions you need.

While input flooding helps with learning up to a point, more complete learning probably happens when you *use* words in many contexts. In other words we can do **Output Flooding** too. You can *use* the new things you are learning until they really stick.

Children, again, when first learning, naturally just listen for quite a while. This is called their 'silent period'. Then they start to use language with great amounts of repetition almost without end (which drives parents crazy sometimes!). Adults, too, may need a certain silent period in the beginning. Then they also need to find ways to do output flooding as well.

The last chapter was about SPURRing new material, finding ways to Use it in Specifically Personal ways, Repeatedly Recycled. But after learning this, you still need to remember to use the material. The following list is what one group of students and I came up with to help ourselves. (I'm learning other languages, too!)

The beauty of such a list is that it allows you to experiment with different ways to incorporate language. The list allows you to choose strategies that you find appealing. You may want to experiment with ones that you think would never work for you. Challenge yourself!

BRAINSTORMING

How we can Select and Register input, and then do Input and Output Flooding, for more intensive language learning and acquisition:

Answers from participants in Murphey's LA & NLP 10/95

SELECTION

1. asking myself, "Can I see myself ever using that word/phrase/expression?"
2. what I have to learn for a test
3. what's funny and fun and useful
4. if I hear it or see it often in a short while, my curiosity light goes on, and flashes GRAB IT!
5. if I notice I want to say something often and I don't know how, I ask how and then select it for use
6. things my classmates use but I don't
7. feel-good words like 'great' and 'wonderful'
8. asking many people the same questions, and selecting the repeated elements for learning

REGISTRATION

1. taking **notes** on paper, word cards, on my hand
2. walking around with a **recording device** (recording me or an informant)
3. repeating silently in my head
4. flashing the picture of the word in my mind
5. writing it 5 times on my hand with my magic finger-pen
6. folding the pages of books to look at again later
7. think of who you can use the word or expression with (future pacing)
8. make an interesting sentence (funny, sexy, etc.) If I laugh I know I can remember it 'cause I will share it later
9. underline or highlight words in a passage - transfer later to cards or Walkman

INPUT FLOODING

1. rereading my notes at special times, on a train, before sleep, when I get up
2. looking at my word cards, attaching them to my key ring
3. listening to same song recorded many times on the same short tape
4. listening to the same conversation, or word list
5. my bathroom has very stylish wallpaper with various vocab lists, key phrases, etc.
6. wearing something, doing something to make people ask about it

OUTPUT FLOODING

1. tell my girl/boyfriend everything I'm learning
2. trying to tell my conversation partners the same stories
3. steering partners toward certain situations where I can use the vocab I'm studying
4. making ten sentences with a new word or expression
5. writing a story with new words and expressions
6. tell each of my family members the same story individually and separately
7. tell everybody my saying for the week (e.g. 'Use it or lose it.')
8. practice different greetings and questions with everybody for a few days at a time: *How are you? What's up? Howzit going?*

MIXED INPUT–OUTPUT FLOODING

1. talking to myself (dialogues, stories, expressions, describing what's around me)
2. singing songs to myself
3. using new words and expressions with a partner who shadows and uses my words.

REMEMBERING TO DO INPUT/OUTPUT FLOODING

1. upside down watch (anchors), cards on your key ring, put your ring on other hand
2. read daily/weekly target words each morning
3. have a special friend that asks me each day what I'm learning
4. associate new words to numbers 1—10, and each time I see a number I recall the word
5. associate new expressions using colours with the actual colours you see. You see green for example and remember "green with envy".
6. associate character words (eg. 'angel') to classmates and friends, and each time I see them I think of the expression.

CHAPTER 20
Good Students Make
Good Teachers

CHAPTER 20
Good Students Make Good Teachers

"We are continually faced with a series of great opportunities brilliantly disguised as insolubile problems"
John W. Gardner

A teacher of mine once did an experiment in class. She came to class and said, "Today you have to tell me what to do and how to change. I will do my best to do as you say." Then she just sat there.

Finally, one student said, "Teach us."

She asked, "How?"

"Talk to us," another said.

So she began talking in a very soft voice. "Could you speak a little louder, please?" someone asked, and she did, but she was speaking too fast and someone said, "A little slower, please," and she slowed down. What she was talking about was not very interesting, so finally, someone said, "Tell us about when you were a student."

So she told an interesting story about how when she had gone to school she had thought that she was a prisoner and that she just had to be there and learn as best she could. She had thought she could not really change anything. Teachers were going to talk and do exactly as they wanted, and the students didn't have any power. Then, one day, one of her teachers came to class and did an experiment. The teacher said, "Today you have to tell me what to do and how to change. I will do my best to do as you say." Then she just sat there ...

So I understood that my teacher wanted more feedback from me so that she could teach better. She wanted to show me that I *could* change things. She helped me to be a proactive learner, someone who took control of their own learning.

If you have teachers who you would like to understand better (in any language), you can become a proactive learner and do many things to improve the situation:

1. **Tell the teacher when you don't understand, and give specific information.** Teachers want to be understood. They will be happy if, when you don't understand, you tell them. Of course *how* you tell them is important. Just saying, "I don't understand," may only frustrate the teacher. Asking for specific changes helps a lot. For example, "I can't hear you very well. Could you speak a bit louder, please?" or, "I didn't understand why we did the last exercise; will you please explain?" or, "What does that word mean?"

When students ask such questions, the teacher knows how to answer and knows what to do. The teacher also knows that the student is really interested.

2. **Ask the teacher to repeat more slowly.** Foreign teachers are used to this request; they will usually gladly do so and they will thank you for letting them know you want to hear it again. And sometimes teachers forget, and so you can remind them again to slow down. It helps to do this in a positive way: "That sounds interesting – could you say it again more slowly, please?"

3. Record your teachers when they speak. Just ask beforehand if it is all right to record. Usually they will be flattered and they will find this a good idea. Just get a little Walkman, turn it on, and leave it on the teacher's desk during the class. After class you can listen to the parts you need as many times as you like. See Chapter 10 for more information about this. Some students have said that this has saved them!

4. Ask other classmates for help. Sit beside a helpful student and read their notes, or ask them for explanations and a copy of their notes after class. Explaining what happened in the class is a good exercise for the student too, because they can learn the material more deeply by telling it to you. So help them out and ask them to tell you about it.

5. Telephone classmates. In many classes, teachers pass around a list of the students with their telephone numbers. Use it! (Or you can ask classmates for their numbers.) Call your friends and ask them – in English preferably! – to tell you again what you did in class. Again, your friends will learn a lot when you ask them to tell you.

6. Go and see the teacher. Although teachers are busy, they usually enjoy seeing you once in a while. If you have

specific questions or wish to ask them to do something different, go and see them in their office. If you think it might take more than a few minutes, then after class ask them for an appointment.

7. Prepare material before you go to the class. When you prepare beforehand (by reading the chapters, etc), then, when you are in class, the material is easier to understand. Most teachers will tell you what you should read or do before the classes so that you will be better prepared.

8. Take notes! Usually it's a good idea to write down everything that the teacher puts on the board. In addition to writing down important points you hear, you probably also want to write down some things you don't understand and questions you might want to ask later. You can also take notes when you talk to classmates.

9. Make eye contact with your teacher and let your face show that you need him or her to slow down or explain more. Teachers like to teach to people who look at them. This also allows the teacher to see if you understand or not, so that they can adjust.

10. Nod when you understand, and stop when you don't. This signal is very important to teachers. Nodding is a positive signal of understanding and tells teachers you are with them. When they've got used to this and you then stop nodding, then they tend to repeat, slow down, and explain in another way. (Of course nodding is very different from nodding off!)

11. When you make eye contact and nod, it is also nice to smile. When you stop smiling, it is also a signal for more explanation. Your smile can put the teacher in a good mood and make learning much more fun!

12. Tell teachers when you really like something, and you'll get more of it. This won't always work, but often it will. Teachers are human; they like compliments, and they also want to please you. Saying something like, "I like the notes you've put on the board today," will probably get the teacher to put more notes on the board in the future. Saying, "Thanks for speaking slowly," will get them to do this more, as well.

Remember, **you are responsible for your education.** If it's not understandable and pleasurable, take actions to change the situation. Be a proactive student. Learn all you can. Take control of your learning environment, and **become a passionate learner!**

CHAPTER 21
Three Things You Need to Succeed: Want To, Know How To, Chance To

CHAPTER 21
Three Things You Need to Succeed: Want To, Know How To, Chance To

"I have no particular talent. I am merely extremely inquisitive."
Albert Einstein

Think about it first!
1. What three things do you think you need in order to learn anything?

Basically there are three ingredients for learning almost anything:

1. You need to **WANT TO** learn. That's called motivation. You need to believe that you can really learn and want to learn.
2. You need to **KNOW HOW TO** do the thing. This could take some time. You may watch some people performing a task, or read books, or listen to someone talk about **how** it is done.
3. You need a **CHANCE TO** actually do it. If you can't try to do it, then you will probably never really learn it. Of course, you can't do it perfectly the first time. *It's trying to do it that teaches you how to do it.*

These three things will help you to learn almost any subject or skill. Let's take juggling as an example:

1. If you don't **want** to learn, it's going to be really hard to get you to do it. (Fortunately, when people first get hold of the juggling balls they usually get interested in learning.)
2. While wanting to learn will give you determination, **knowing** a few basic steps will usually make learning happen a lot faster and more smoothly.
3. Of course, the crucial thing is that you have a **chance** to throw the balls around, and drop them, and learn through the act of juggling. You may need to do this in private for a while. So I loan balls to students to take home and experiment with. *Doing it teaches you how to do it.*

Want To, Know How To and Chance To are not really three steps, but three things that go hand in hand. If you are lacking in one, the others tend to suffer. For example, without a chance to actually do it, the motivation and the level of learning can go down. This is basically what happens in schools, where students seldom have the **chance to** actually use English to interact because most teachers don't use English as the language of the classroom. You are more motivated when you can actually **USE** what you are learning in your everyday life.

How are you doing?
How much WANT TO do you have?
None   1 2 3 4 5 6 7 8 9 10 A lot
How much KNOW HOW?
None   1 2 3 4 5 6 7 8 9 10 A lot
How much CHANCE TO?
None   1 2 3 4 5 6 7 8 9 10 A lot

Where are you a little low?
What would happen if you had more of it?
Where can you find it?
What three things could you do to improve the situation?
Who is responsible for improving the situation?

"WANT TO"   **"KNOW HOW TO"**   **"CHANCE TO"**

Crucial desire

I've noticed that I can teach students a lot about how they can learn (eg. shadowing, reformulation, and memory strategies). And I can give them chances to practise, and tell them how they can make more opportunities to practise outside the classroom (*Try a Non-native*, *Use your Walkman*, etc).

Sometimes showing students good strategies makes them want to learn, and their desire catches fire. Sometimes when I can persuade them to try self-talk ("Sounds crazy doesn't it? Sure does. But it works!") students find that they can improve much more just by talking to themselves. It's amazing and it creates more desire to find more ways to increase their learning. So sometimes Know How To and Chance To can lead to Want To.

Notice also, though, that teaching inappropriate Know How To and Chance To can deflate Want To. If you want to learn to juggle and I try to teach you the physics and mathematical formulas for curves and gravitation, it may bore you. Or if I give you five balls to start with, and then say, "Go home and practise (Chance To) for two hours a day," your motivation will go down (along with the balls) under the weight of frustration. So when teachers try to explain grammar rules that even native speakers can't understand, it's little wonder that some of their students don't want to continue learning. David McClelland, a Harvard psychologist, originally came up with the conceptualization of Want To, Know How To, and Chance To. Through the use of questionnaires and analysis, he found that he could tell if a person needed motivation, training, or changes in the system. This last could mean something like an educational system needing to give more opportunities to learners to use the language for real communication.

When you want to learn fast, desire is crucial. A simple wish is not enough. When you want it with all your heart, you get so much more – it's exciting to learn! When you are excited and really want to learn something, you can overcome small upsets and you work through problems with more determination.

Language learning is a long-term task with ups and downs and struggles at times (the roller coaster of progress). If you have only a wish, it's hard to overcome the occasional difficulties. But a deeply felt desire to learn and to become all you can be makes you powerful. This desire makes you more powerful than your mistakes do, or even your grades. When you really want to learn, you don't just work for grades – you work for yourself. You want to become as wonderful as you can become. And then you have a better gift to give to others, and you can help them even more.

The structure of desire

Some people think that either you like something or you don't. I used to be that way, but then I found out that I could play with my brain and pretend to love things that I didn't like but were good for me. For example, my older brother told me some pretty terrible things about tomatoes when I was a kid, and I hated them for a while. Then it dawned on me that they were just another vegetable and that to a certain extent I could decide what tasted good or bad. I started slowly at first, just a bite, saying, "This is delicious!" Then I started associating all kinds of wonderful things with tomatoes (for example, good health, my girlfriend, etc). And now I'm a tomato freak!

When you really want to turn on your desire and feel excited about studying something, it helps to find others who already feel that way, and then just do what they do. To a great extent this is something that you decide. And once you have decided, then you allow your passion to grow! Then other things just begn to happen. Test this out. Tell yourself that you feel passionate about something, and then see how your desire increases and how your brain begins to think of ways to do whatever it is you want to do. Please don't just accept this – use your mind as a laboratory, and find out for yourself!

Below are the chapters and activities in this book. Which ones do you think are **mostly** concerned with WANT TO (W), or KNOW HOW TO (K), or CHANCE TO (C)? (Of course all of them contain bits of all three and some a lot of all three.)

Write W, K, or C beside each heading:

1. The Roller Coaster of Your Language Learning
2. Try a Non-native!
3. Appreshiating Misteakes
4. Shadowing, Summarizing and Self-Talk
5. A Teddy Bear in Your Ear
6. Remember your Memory … It's What You Make It
7. Serious FUN
8. Learned Genkiness
9. Friendly Watching and Upside Downing Time
10. Just You and Your Walkman
11. Everyone's a Juggler!
12. Brain Play I: On Second Thought
13. Brain Play II: Fun with Junkthought
14. Focusing on Attention: Where is Your Seven plus or minus Two?
15. Passion, Vision, and Action
16. Your Specific Successes
17. Collaboration: When Students Learn Most
18. From Learned Helplessness to SPURR
19. Input and Output Flooding
20. Good Students Make Good Teachers
21. Want To, Know How To, Chance To
22. Being Language Hungry

Appendices

1. Once Upon a Time …
2. Reminders * Think about it, then DO IT!
3. Beliefs Inventory
4. Brain Play Summary
5. Songs and Jazz Chants
6. Juggling Manga

CHAPTER 22
Being Language Hungry

CHAPTER 22
Being Language Hungry!

Think about it first!
1. Describe who you are; write it down in a few sentences. Then at the end of this chapter go back to it and see if you want to change anything.
2. What beliefs do you have most of the time about your ability to learn?

Language hungry. That was the only way I could describe her.

When I asked her how she had learned English so well without leaving Japan, she simply said, "All you have to do is pretend. Pretend you are an English speaker." She said she first got hooked on pop music in English in junior high school. Along the way she developed a knack for finding and imitating English everywhere she went. She confessed she used to listen to the English radio programs with her earphone even while she was in other classes. Her radar was always on full alert for English. Wherever she heard it, she would listen and repeat whatever she heard, finding her automatic repeating button always "on".

Later, English would just come flowing back through her head like a pleasant dream. She pretended she was the actresses in the movies she saw, and often gestured with them when they talked. She even read MacDonald cups. She told me, "You know, English is everywhere when you really want it. You may not control the external environment as much as you would like, but you are in control of the internal one. And you can tune your own brain into any channel you want, at any time." And now she was a teacher, trying to show her students how to become English Hungry. (Journal entry, Oct. 10, 1994)

Logical Levels of Learning

Anthropologist Gregory Bateson identified four basic levels of learning and change. The higher the level, the more impact on the individual. (Dilts, 1994) Bateson's levels roughly correspond to these five:

a. Who I **A**m – Identity   Who?
b. My **B**elief System – Values and Meanings   Why?
c. My **C**apabilities – Strategies and States   How?
d. What I **D**o or Have **D**one – Specific types of Behaviour What?
e. My **E**nvironment – External Constraints   Where? When?

For students, they might translate into something similar to this:

            *   I **am** (not) an English speaker. **Identity**
        *   *   It's good (bad) to speak English. **Beliefs**
    *   *   *   I (don't) know how to speak English. **Capability**
  *   *   *   *   I (don't) do what my teacher says. **Behaviour**
*   *   *   *   *   School is part of my **Environment.**

Starting from the bottom and going up, we could say that students go to school and are in a certain **Environment**. In this environment we hope to cultivate certain types of **Behaviour**. Sometimes when students behave in a certain way for long enough they develop the strategies and states that give them the **Capability** to reproduce language regularly. Other students can produce the required types of behaviour only in the contexts in which they are learned – in school and at exams. Still other students can't even do that.

Notice that we may get students to behave a certain way in a classroom, yet often this does not become a capability, a skill, that is used outside the classroom. Notice also that students can acquire skills at a certain level – yet if they don't have the supporting beliefs that, for example, the skills are worthwhile or that speaking English is good, the skills probably won't become well developed and used outside the school.

In my own teaching, I have often operated (unconsciously mostly) on the idea that good **Beliefs** could help language learners most. I've tried to help students believe 'English is fun and good to learn' and 'Mistakes are helpful' and 'People want to talk to me', so that students would learn with more enthusiasm and energy.

Recently, I've become more aware of the power of **Identity** and how it facilitates changes at the lower levels. Let me tell you of a few experiences:

* A few times a year I go to international conferences, so I get Japanese teachers to run a few classes in my absence with the materials and the routines that I have prepared beforehand. I ask them to speak only English to the class and they do. Inevitably when I return I read in my students' action logs (Murphey 1993) that they were very impressed with the Japanese teacher who spoke only English and that they realized that perhaps one day they would be able to speak like her. The weeks following the substitute teacher's presence are usually ones in which my students' enthusiasm expands, and the vitality is wonderful. (I sometimes think maybe I should go away more often.)

* Recently my seminar students have been conducting some of their research using my first-year students. The older students present their topics and questionnaires in English, calmly and clearly. Again, the first-year students are impressed with the older students' English, courage, and willingness to make mistakes in front of a large group. They express a belief that perhaps one day they will speak like the older students.

* At the JALT 94 conference in Matsuyama, I met a Japanese high school teacher whose English was so great, I asked her how many years she had been abroad. She replied that she had never been abroad and she told me basically the story at the beginning of this article – that she had simply become 'English hungry'. I told my students briefly about this woman. Again, nearly all remarked in their action logs that they had always thought you had to go live abroad in order to really learn to communicate in English. And here was a real Japanese who spoke fluently, who had even become a teacher, who had never been abroad. Maybe, my students reasoned, they didn't have to wait to go abroad to really learn English. If one person could do it here in Japan, others could, too.

What the reactions from my students have helped me to realize is that they need role models, people who they can identify with more closely than foreign teachers. When they see, or even hear of, someone with whom they can identify easily (someone who resembles them in some way), and this person has fluent English as part of their identity, then they find it easier to adopt the phrase 'I am an English speaker' or at least the belief 'I can become an English speaker'. Changes in behaviour and capabilities then become easier because they are supported by an ideal future self.

Learners need near-peer role models (Murphey & Arao, 2001), people who are fairly similar to them and whom they admire and want to be more like. Near-peer role models keep motivation high and allow learners to imagine their ideal self. They allow learners to join an imagined community of people like themselves who can speak and use the target language (Murphey, Chen, & Chen, 2005).

Naturally if all the levels are working together then great things can happen. However there are often contradictions that you can hear, things like, 'I am Xyz (identity) and Xyzs don't learn foreign languages well (limiting belief). It's good to know languages (belief) but I can't speak very well (capability).' Contrast this to 'I am a Xyz who is also a foreign language speaker and user (identity). Foreign languages are fun and interesting (belief). I can make myself understood in most situations (capability) and if I make a mistake, it's okay – I don't have to be perfect (belief).'

Although it may seem almost too simple, say to yourself right now, 'I'm a foreign language speaker' three times (in the foreign language, of course), and just pretend it's true – play with your brain. If you play sincerely, you'll find that you value yourself more, think you are more capable, behave as though you are more capable and thus seek out more moments in your environment to speak your foreign language. Many of you realize already that this is the structure of self-fulfilling prophecies. Say you can't, and you don't try, and you prove yourself correct. Pretend you can, and you do try. Through trying repeatedly, you interact and so find ways to learn and become what you pretend. Richard Bach put it most succinctly when he said in *Illusions* 'Argue for your limitations, and sure enough, they're yours' (p 75). Kurt Vonnegut completed

Bach's idea, in his introduction to *Mother Night*, 'We are what we pretend to be, so we must be careful about what we pretend to be.' (p v)

Please don't believe anything I've said in this chapter. I would much prefer you to try it out on yourself and observe what happens. Let that be your test of the information. Just play with your own brain and notice what happens in your own world, your own mind. Think of a model, be that person for a moment – then see how you feel, and notice what you say to yourself and what you feel like doing.

A version of this chapter was originally published as 'Identity and Beliefs in Language Learning' in JALT's *The Language Teacher* 19(4) 34—36 (April 1995)

Bach, Richard (1977) *Illusions*. London: Mandarin.

Dilts, Robert (1994) *Effective Presentation Skills* Capitola, CA: Meta Publications.

Murphey, T. & Arao, H. (2001). 'Changing Reported Beliefs through Near Peer Role Modeling'. *TESL-EJ.* 5(3)1—15. Accessed at http://www-writing.berkeley.edu/TESL-EJ/ej19/a1.html

Murphey, Tim (1993) 'Why don't teachers learn what learners learn? Taking the guesswork out with action logging.' *English Teaching Forum* January pp 6—10.

Murphey, Tim; Chen, Jin; & Chen, Li-Chi (2005). 'Learners' constructions of identities and imagined communities.' In P. Benson & D. Nunan (eds.), *Learners' Stories: Difference and Diver-sity in Language Learning* pp83—100. Cambridge: Cambridge University Press.

Vonnegut, Kurt (1966) *Mother Night*. New York: Dell Publishing Co.

TEACHER NOTES
How to Use *Language Hungry!*
Suggestions for teachers
(and everyone can be a teacher)

TEACHER NOTES
How to Use *Language Hungry!*
Suggestions for teachers (and everyone can be a teacher)

Who uses *Language Hungry!?*

Language Hungry! (LH) has been used by teachers and students around the world in many different ways. I have used LH to teach all levels at university and graduate school with native and non-native speakers, as well as teachers in training. Colleagues have used it in junior colleges, high schools, technical schools, and in one-to-one teaching. The point is that the information in this book is mostly independent of level and language; the English may be at the intermediate level but the ideas are useful for everyone, anytime. In fact, teachers tell me that one of the reasons they like it so much is that they improve their own learning when they are teaching the ideas in LH.

The flexible order of the chapters

The chapters are not built on each other, and can be read in any order. In my own classes, I tend to skip around in a different way each year as I get to know the students and so can work out what they need at any particular time.

So please read the entire book yourself first, and then because you know your students you'll be able to decide on the order you think would best suit them. You will probably, too, have a preferred teaching style and you can pick from the chapters to make the most of this. A colleague of mine often starts with Chapter 17 when she sees it is important that her students deal first with the limiting belief of shyness. She also thinks it especially important for students to compare themselves only with themselves and to learn to collaborate early on. Another teacher often chooses to start with juggling (Chapter 11) because he feels it is such a good metaphor for the whole

learning process.

Another way to decide the order is to ask the students to 'make friends with the book' (see box on p142). You can ask them which chapters look the most interesting to them. Then follow their interests and enthusiasm.

Whatever order you decide on, remember that you can change whenever you see the need.

Ways you can use LH

LH is being used by some teachers as a main text and by others as an auxiliary one. There are many ways to use it. Text in **Bold** below shows how I use it most of the time.

Before students read

· You can talk about the topic in class. This makes the reading much easier. Showing that you personally are excited about the ideas also helps!

· **It is especially helpful to get students to ask the *Think about it first!* questions to each other,** because this helps them recall knowledge that they already possess. This usually makes it easier for them to read the new material and to remember it. Hanging new knowledge onto the hook of the existing is the way that our brains work.

· Ask the students to keep a log of their personal experiences and their reactions to each chapter. These can be shared with their classmates regularly or periodically.

While students read

· LH can be a supplementary text for extensive reading. Because it is highly interesting to students, they may well be able to do this quickly, and so be encouraged.

· Certain parts of the book can be read in

pairs in class, the students taking turns shadowing each other and then summarizing the main points.

After students read they can talk more ...
· Telephone a classmate to tell them what they think of the chapter. This could be their partner that day. Or you can create a class list: ask students to write their names and phone numbers on it, then copy it and distribute it. Then, the first time, ask each student to call the first person below them (the last person calls the first). For the next homework they call the second person below them, and so on.
When students can talk to somebody about the text, it increases their understanding greatly; they learn that talking about things helps them understand that their partners can help them, and that they can help their partners.
· Talk about it in class with classmates and with you (preferably after having read and written about it for homework).
· **Do experiments with an idea.** Try self-talk, shadowing, NNS conversations etc. after reading parts (or all). Then write feedback, or report orally on how it worked – or didn't!
· **Compare their own learning strategies and emotions with those they read about** (do this in discussion, or in writing). This of course combines all four basic skills, and develops metacognition – thinking about thinking.
· **After students read they can write more ...**
· After reading a chapter, or several, react to what they've read in writing. **You can ask them: "Briefly summarize the main points, and express your opinion about the ideas."**
· Write reports and letters on their personal experiences with the ideas, then send them to me (Google on 'Tim Murphey', or contact Helbling) so that the next edition can perhaps include their findings, stories and experiences.

· **Write or record a summary of LH and their experiences in trying out the ideas.** After finishing the book, students can write about how they have changed their learning strategies and behaviours. For example, in 2004, Akinori Seki's class at Niigata Women's College produced a complete book in Japanese; in it, different students summarized different chapters of LH and described how they personally used the ideas. Another class produced a CD in English and Japanese, summarizing the main ideas.
· **Write their language-learning histories** with reference to the ideas in LH.

How you actually use the book is up to you and your students.
While I've included some suggestions for each chapter, I do suggest that you ask your students for input. Adjust to their ability and their interests. Invite them to read this section, or explain it to them. Then ask them to tell you what they think would be the most interesting way for them to use the book.

Making friends with the book
· When your students first get the book, you might ask them to do the 'photo-reading technique' of turning a page every two seconds at a steady pace until they have gone all the way through it. Ask them to keep a 'soft focus' on the pages and just pick up words and pictures as they go along. After they've done that, tell them, "Great – your mind has already read the book. You've finished it once. So now you know it, in a way."
· Then they can tell their partners what they think of the book, and what they found interesting. This allows them to make friends with the book from the outset.
· **Tip:** Invite students to put their own name and phone number on the first page.

ACTIVITIES AND IDEAS, CHAPTER BY CHAPTER

Preface and Introduction

· Ask your students to summarize to each other how the book was made. What part did students play in its creation?

· Ask your students what are the most important suggestions made in the introduction and why might these be important.

1. The Roller Coaster of your Language Learning

· Ask students to draw a few roller coasters of their own learning, including one starting from when they began, spanning perhaps years, and ending in the present moment.

· Ask students to compare their roller coasters with those of their classmates, and ask each other what made their roller coasters go up or down.

2. Try a Non-native

· Ask students to make a list of non-native speakers in their out-of-school environment who they could use the target language with and learn from. Ask them to share this list with a partner and explain who their potential language-learning partners are.

· Ask students to exchange phone numbers and to telephone each other in English and speak in English on the telephone. They need only describe what they are doing at the moment and what they did that day and perhaps what they plan to do after ending the phone call. Or you can give them more appropriate questions suited to their interests and levels.

3. Appreshiating Misteakes

· Ask students to write down a short story about a mistake they made and bring it to class for others to read.

· Ask them to tell their stories in pairs, changing partners every five minutes.

4. Shadowing, Summarizing and Self-talk

· Ask students to experiment with shadowing and summarizing in their other classes, and then, working in small groups, to report to one another how it works.

· Ask students to experiment with shadowing and summarizing a radio or TV programme and to report back to their classmates how it went.

5. A Teddy Bear in your Ear

· Ask your students, singly or in pairs, to bring you a recording of a favourite song in the target language and a copy of the lyrics. Out of class, select those that look and sound interesting to the other students. Make copies of the lyrics, having put a small strip of paper down the middle to block out several letters at a time. Students can try to fill in the blanks before they listen, then while they listen, and then compare with classmates after listening. Many songs also present good discussion topics.

· See *Music and Song* (Tim Murphey, 1992, OUP) for many other activities that can be used to enhance language learning.

6. Remember your memory ... It's What You Make It

· As a warm-up to this chapter, or after reading it, show your students a Mind Map of that day's class activities on a projector or poster, or on the board, and ask them to tell each other what they understand from it.

· Ask your students to make a list of words they want to learn better and to write them into a bizarre story. Then ask them to tell the story to friends, without looking at their papers. Follow this up by asking them if the strangeness of the story helped them remember the new words. Usually it does, and then the students become convinced that this method of learning will be effective for them.

7. Serious FUN

• Ask students to tell each other in pairs or small groups when and where they play the most and have fun the most.

• Then ask them to imagine how studying would be for them if they found it really playful. Ask them to tell you what would need to be changed about studying to make it more fun.

8. Learned Genkiness

• Ask students if they have ever learned to be helpless and passive about anything, and then to explain it to a partner. For example, 'My first-grade teacher criticized a tree I drew, and I 'learned' that I could not draw. I felt that way for many years. But now I love drawing, and learning more about how to draw, and I have abandoned the idea that I can't draw.' Ask them what 'I can't' beliefs they might challenge within themselves.

• Accepting mistakes and frustration is part of learning. So, incorporate into your lesson plans some time for a certain amount of failure, and give yourself permission and time to make the mistakes and learn from them. Specific goals and time frames are important. This is related to Chapter 3 on mistakes and Chapter 16 on making your goals specific.

9. Friendly Watching and Upside Downing Time

• Get a map of the world, or your country, or continent, and hang it upside down in your classroom or office. Then generate discussion on how being on top or on the bottom changes our perspective.

• Create a backwards day, and invite students to wear their shirts inside out.

10. Just You and your Walkman

• For a short while at the beginning of class, listen to a recording through headphones; do not tell your students what you are listening to. Then get them to talk about what you were doing. Ask them to tell partners how much they use a Walkman, and for what purposes.

• Ask students to contribute recordings for a class cassette, CD, or MiniDisk. These could be around a theme like 'valuable things I have learned in class' or 'advice for life'.

11. Everyone's a Juggler!

• Ask students to write down a list of things they have studied or learned. Ask them to choose one, and to think about the beliefs they had/have while learning, and their emotions, their strategies, how their levels change(d) or not, and what steps were involved.

• Then ask them to compare what they have found with their language learning. How are they similar? What beliefs, emotions, and strategies do they find useful in language learning?

12. Brain Play I: On Second Thought

• Ask students to fill out an ABCD chart about their own 'happenings', and then to brainstorm the other students' thoughts, emotions and behaviours about those things.

• Invite students to visualize themselves at some time in the future speaking well and smoothly. Ask them to see all the things in the pictures and hear what is going on. Then ask them to describe their picture to a partner.

13. Brain Play II: Fun with Junkthought

• Place a chart on the wall with the four junkthoughts, and when one comes up gently point to it, to show students that these really do occur in everyday life.

• Ask students to bring examples of junkthoughts that they find in their daily lives, through reading or listening to others.

14. Focusing on Attention: Where is your Seven plus or minus Two?

• To incorporate the information in this

chapter, give students a short list of vocabulary or idioms and ask them to memorize them, applying the concepts in this chapter.

· Ask them to write a short report, for other students to read, on the learning experience they had through using these techniques.

15. Passion, Vision, and Action

· Ask students to list a set of goals they had when they were younger, and to evaluate them according to clarity of vision, the degree of passion, and the amount of action they needed to accomplish the goals.

· Ask students to give examples of people in their environment who have above average vision, passion, and action.

16. Your Specific Successes

· Ask students to make a list of goals for the coming semester or year, and then to check to see if they fit the criteria of PC SERSEF.

· Ask them to discuss with partners which criteria they think are most important. Ask which ones they seem to have disregarded in the past so maybe should pay more attention to.

17. Collaboration: When Students Learn Most from Each Other

· Ask students to discuss with their classmates which of the four myths they might have believed, or still do believe.

· Ask them to discuss how people change from shy to talkative, and what is needed for them to be talkative.

18. From Learned Helplessness to SPURR

· Ask students to turn to the chart at the end of this chapter, and put a tick beside the strategies they use, then to compare and discuss these with their partners. How much are they using which kinds of strategies?

· Ask students to choose a few A-student strategies that they do not currently use, try them out for a few days and then report back to the class on how they went. You may have to give them some corresponding assignments so they can try out the new ways of learning.

19. Input and Output Flooding

· Ask students to gather a small amount of material that they wish to learn. Invite them to discuss their choices with their partners: are their choices appropriate, too few, too much, at the right level? What other questions did they ask themselves to decide to learn the item?

· Ask them to discuss how they registered the material they want to learn. What is in writing, recorded, or simply in their minds? Were there things they missed and could not register?

· Invite them to tell their partners which input and output strategies they would like to use to learn the material. How will they remember to do the input and output flooding? Ask them to report in a few days' time what's happened.

20. Good Students Make Good Teachers

· Invite students to discuss how much interaction they have with their other teachers in other classes, perhaps without using any specific names. Eg: "My history teacher says Hello to me every time I see her." Discuss how they could have more interaction that might help them.

· Ask them to discuss with their classmates whether they are making their teachers' teaching easier or more difficult, and how they could help their teachers more.

21. Want To, Know How To, Chance To

· Ask students to describe how much their past teachers provided Want To (motivation), Know How To (information), and Chance To (opportunities to use the language).

· Ask students to discuss how they could provide these things when they are lacking in a course.

22. Being Language Hungry

• Ask students to say to themselves, silently in their heads, over and over again, "I am an English speaker" (or "Je suis francophone" etc. in the language being studied). Ask them to describe to a partner how it makes them feel. How much does it motivate them to want to study more?

• Ask students which of the Logical Levels of Learning (identity, beliefs, capabilities, behaviour, environment) they think they can act on and control the most, and why.

• Ask students to believe "something impossible" (like the White Queen in *Alice Through the Looking-Glass*) just for a while and to dream that they speak the target language fluently and perfectly. When they believe this, what else changes? Ask them to notice and to report to others.

Providing near-peer role models for your students: an action plan for teachers

To get the students in your class to inspire each other, I suggest the following.

1. Start by telling your students stories of successful language learners who are as close to their own experiences as possible – the same country, region, sex, age, school, teacher, original distaste for school, hobbies, dreams. A metaphor that's effective for someone is one that has a structure similar to their real-life concerns. I remember that in my small rural high school they used to bring back successful graduates to give talks about how to succeed in life. What was impressive was not so much what they said as the fact that they'd once been to our high school and had ended up successful – – that helped us feel that we could do it too.

Then, after you've told a story, give the students a few minutes to reformulate the story in pairs, to tell each other what they have understood and to add their opinions. I find that doing this helps them to encode the story much more deeply in their minds, and it becomes a more powerful motivator.

Also, those who haven't quite understood often do understand more clearly when it's explained to them personally by a classmate.

2. If you're teaching in a country foreign to you, ask a native of that country who's a speaker of the language you're teaching to do some short presentations in your classroom. Again, the more similar these speakers are to your students, the easier it is for them to identify with them.

3. If you're a non-native speaking (NNS) teacher of a target language, you are potentially the most powerful role model **when you speak the target language in your own classes.** When you show you enjoy speaking it and even allow yourself to make a few mistakes, students receive the message that the language is pleasurable and that we don't have to be perfect to speak it. But if, on the other hand, you speak mostly your native language in class, you are sending out meta-messages such as: "The foreign language is not for speaking, just analysis" and "Even I don't speak it," and, "I don't have the confidence that I can communicate effectively with you in the target language" and even, "I'm afraid to speak it because you have to be perfect like the tapes."

I feel strongly about this last point. If we could magically incorporate the phrase 'I am an effective speaker of the foreign language' into the identity of NNS teachers, the power of their model would greatly help their students. This factor alone, rather than increasing the number of native speakers, is what would make positive changes in educational systems. The goal of a language learner is not to become a native speaker, but instead to become something much more achievable – an effective user of the language.

I know there are already some excellent NNS role models out there, because I've met them. When they teach in the target language, students realise much more of their potential; they are challenged to be all that they can be. And we need teachers who will bring to life Gandhi's words: "Be the change you wish to see in the world."

APPENDICES

APPENDIX 1
Once Upon A Time ...
a few stories to think about

Short Story 1 : *The Wait Watcher*

I had a nice friend once – a rather large lady friend. In fact, she was so large that you really couldn't get close enough to kiss her on the cheek.

Well, once she decided to go on a diet and do exercise to lose weight. On TV they have regular aerobics and exercise classes. You can turn on the TV every morning and watch aerobics. So that's what my friend did. She watched aerobics. Every morning. Trouble is, that's all she did ... watch. She didn't do them, she just watched and hoped some miracle would make her thin. Like the people on TV. Needless to say, she stayed fat.

So I said to her, "You know, if you don't *do* something, you won't *get what you want*. Just watching by itself doesn't help. You have to *do to become* the things you see. And that will make *you feel good*."

So she did. She got so excited about it that she joined a club and four years later she became an aerobics teacher herself.

Short Story 2: *Environmental Engineering – Crazy about French*

When I lived in Florida I met a wonderful person named Joan. The first time I talked to Joan, I thought she was French because that's all she would speak with me. She was crazy about French. In fact, in her apartment she wouldn't speak anything but French. That was her law. She had it written on her door. She wanted to learn French as well as she could, and she couldn't afford to go abroad.

She had French posters on her walls and everything was labelled in French. She only had French songs on her tape player, and she watched French videos. She read French magazines, books and newspapers. She had French bread, served French wine and Perrier, and she really only spoke French when *chez Joan**. When you were with her, you really felt as though you were in France. On the street a lot of people mistook her for French because she often spoke to herself in French, and to others as well. In elevators it was fun to speak French to her about the people around us who couldn't understand.

It was funny when people came to her door. If she didn't want to speak to them (eg salesmen), she would just speak French and they would go away. If she did want to speak to them but they couldn't speak French, she would step out in the hall and speak in English. She had a few French friends, and lots of other friends who found her game interesting and enjoyed going to France *chez Joan* because French with her was enjoyable. She was really very popular. She later even won a scholarship to study abroad because of her efforts.

*chez = 'at the home of'

groups were not so enthusiastic. Why? Because they had been told repeatedly, "Bend your knees and put your weight forward," while my group had played aeroplanes while singing "Wwwaaaahhh!"

The camp director asked himself a few questions: Who is a better ski teacher for beginners? What kind of teacher gets kids hooked on skiing? Which one is better for business? Which is cheaper?

Do you want to learn something? **Make it easy, make it fun. Make it an adventure!**

Short Story 3: *Having Fun Naturally*

When, as a poor student, I first went to Switzerland I had skied for only a few days in my life. For a part-time job at Christmas, I went to a sports camp where I was supposed to be the bus driver. But because they didn't have enough ski teachers, they gave me a beginner group of small children and told me to teach them.

Now, I didn't know much about teaching skiing, but I was good with kids. And I like to have fun. So for those two weeks we played a lot of games on skis, we crashed a lot and we laughed our heads off. We tickled each other a lot and sang songs going up the lifts. And we had adventures.

At the end of the two weeks a skiing competition was held for the four beginner classes. I hadn't known about this before. It was on a gentle slope, but the skiers had to make about seven turns and they were timed. All four groups did fairly well, but my kids came in second! I was amazed, and so was the camp director, because the other three groups had had real ski teachers who had taught them a lot of techniques.

But the real test came when the director asked the children if they had enjoyed themselves and wanted to come back for more ski camps. My group had loved skiing and definitely wanted to come back for another camp, but the other three

Short Story 4: *Playing the Game: Tennis On and Off the Court*

For a year I went to a small junior college in North Carolina. To fulfil the physical education requirement during the first term, the school offered either tennis or ballroom dancing. For me the choice was clear. In the fall, I took tennis class and played tennis for the first time.

The first day, the teacher just let us play as we liked. We thought "Great!" and decided we might like him. We got onto the court and tried hitting the balls to each other. But we were lucky if we hit the ball twice before it went over the fence or onto the next court. Most of our time was spent chasing balls, so we got very frustrated.

After that first class, we thought the course was going to be boring and that the teacher was really no good at all. But in the next class, things changed. The teacher asked us if we liked tennis. Nobody raised their hand. He said he understood, and he agreed that it sometimes is frustrating, especially if you try too hard too soon.

"Now," he said, "I hope you see why a little instruction might help you. Because it really is a fun game. But just chasing balls isn't. Now I'm going to try to teach you by showing you how enjoyable t is, through a lot of different exercises."

And he did. We had relay races bouncing the balls off our rackets. He taught us how to play at the net, which was easy because all you had to do was meet the ball to send it back. Then he showed us how to hit off walls and to play against ourselves. That day was a lot more fun. At the end of it he said:

"So you see, it can be fun. But I still don't think you will learn much in this class, because we don't meet often enough. If you really want to learn how to play tennis, you have to play the game outside class, and off the court."

Well, that sounded pretty strange. "How can you play tennis off the court?" we thought.

That night I happened to see a tennis game on television in our student dormitory and decided to watch for a while. Later, in bed, before going to sleep, I realized that the game I had watched was running through my mind. But the person I was watching was me. And I was hitting all those beautiful shots, just like the professionals. I was putting myself into the picture. I actually dreamed about tennis all night.

The next tennis class was amazing. I got hooked on tennis. I put the images into my head and let my body do it. When I relaxed I played much better and found I was much more capable. Just to make sure I wasn't fooling myself, I started going to the gym every evening for about a half an hour and I would hit a tennis ball off the wall. I did that all winter. I became a tennis fanatic. I dreamed tennis. Every field I saw, I imagined a tennis court in it. I would think, "Umm, would a court fit in there?" and, "How would it look?" When I was bored in other classes, I would play a game of tennis in my mind.

That spring, I tried out for the tennis team and made it. I started out as the eighth player, and throughout the spring I moved gradually up until by the end of the school year I was the number three player on the team. They even awarded me the award for most valuable player because I had won more matches than anyone else!

Looking back, I now realize what it means to play the game off the court.

Short Story 5: *When the Doctors went on Strike*

In a large American city several years ago, the doctors in the hospitals went on strike. People feared that there would be many deaths since no doctors were at the hospitals to treat ill people. However, the opposite happened: the death rate actually went down; far fewer people died during the strike than at other times. Some people jokingly said, "Medicine can be dangerous for your health." But others explained it another way.

Doctors are often seen as demigods, able to heal us with science and technology. Many people think that their last chance is the hospital. They think, "The doctors will take care of me. The doctors will save me." Because we have such faith in medicine, we don't take very good care of ourselves. We eat too much, and eat too much of the wrong things. We drink and smoke too much. We push ourselves to extremes. But what happens when we think there are no doctors at the hospital?

We may get frightened. So then we think, "We have to take care of ourselves, by ourselves." We start being careful, very careful, because there is no backup. We have to depend only on ourselves. So when the doctors are on strike, we eat better, rest more, drive more carefully, etc.

Why can't we *do this all the time*? No matter how good doctors are, they are not gods. They make mistakes and don't know all the answers. So maybe we should live as if there were no doctors, no backups. We need to take care of ourselves.

This story doesn't mean that doctors and medicine are bad. But it shows that we don't really *do all we can do for ourselves*. In schools, we may waste time waiting for teachers to teach us; and, in life, waiting for people to love us. We need to *be more proactive instead of reactive. Learn and Love Actively!*

Short Story 6: *Getting to the Top – Your Way*

Once, I wanted to climb a rather high mountain in the Alps. I knew it was a little dangerous and I had heard that many people had got lost trying to get to the top. Many of them had given up. But I was convinced I wanted to try.

At the bottom of the mountain was a little café. I stopped there to have a drink and ask for instructions. There were two very experienced mountain climbers at the café who were going up the mountain that very morning. One was an older woman who called herself Ms East. The other was an older man named Mr West.

As we talked, I discovered that they were not really together. It was just by chance that we all had met at the café. Since there were many paths outside the café, I asked them which one I should take. At first they were reluctant to answer. Finally, Mr West said, "Well, after my years of experience, I would say the eastern path should be the safest and most sure. Yes, if I were you I would take the eastern path." Then he got up and started walking up the mountain in the opposite direction, on the western path.

As you can imagine, I thought that was rather strange. So I asked Ms East which path she thought I should take. She hesitated and then finally said, looking at the sky, "With weather like today, I would take the western path. Yes, if I were you I would go west." Then she got up and started to go up – but in the opposite direction. She walked up the eastern path.

Well now, you can imagine I was quite confused. And while I looked first one way and then the other, I noticed a small path leading up the mountain just behind the café. I don't know why, but I decided to try it and see what it was like.

My path was quite a good one for a long while, but then it got smaller and smaller. Finally it wasn't a path at all. I kept climbing. There were cliffs and wild animals, waterfalls and landslides. It wasn't easy, but I didn't like going back, and I had already come such a long way. Finally, I reached the top. I was tired and thirsty and hungry. My clothes were torn and I was bleeding from many scratches. But I was so happy to see the top!

Just as I arrived I saw Mr West arriving from one direction and Ms East from the other. They were smiling at me.

"We see you found the right path," old Ms East said to me.

"Yes," old Mr West echoed, "the very best way indeed, I believe."

Short Story 7: *The Four-year-old Scientist*

I'm sure this will have happened to you as a language learner: You've been away from school or out of the country for a while. You try to remember all the language you knew before you left. And you can't (at least for a while). Nothing comes (well, almost nothing). You are sure that you've forgotten it all. There's a leak somewhere in your brain. What you had so carefully put in has now gone!

As a small child I used to have a favourite glass that I drank all my milk out of. The bottom half was painted blue like the sea, with little fish on it. I used to take the glass out into my garden, fill it with water and then drop some sand into it. With my head beside the glass, I would watch the particles drift slowly to the bottom, out of sight. Then I would put my finger in it, stir it up and watch the pieces swirl up to the top where I could see them again. After a while they would slowly drift down again, out of sight, just like the snow in a glass Christmas bubble. So at the age of four I invented my first physical law of activity: activity (stirring, motion, etc) makes things visible, knowable. **Without activity, the stirring up, we may think there is nothing there any more. But there is.** Usually. It just takes a bit of activity for what is there to come to the surface again. Language is rather like that.

One summer holiday, I forgot my glass of water and sand in the garden. When I came home, I went to see if my theory still worked. I put my finger in and stirred. I found that the sand had become stuck to the sides and that it took more effort, more stirring. Some of it came up in big chunks stuck together, and sank again really fast. Some stayed stuck to the side of the glass for quite a while. So I developed my second law of sand-in-a-glass: **the effort needed to reactivate something will be relative to the length of time of disuse.**

Then one of my brothers gave me a toothbrush, and I used that to unstick the rest of my magic sand and stir up everything that was inside. So I developed my third law of sand-in-a-glass: **other people have information and tools that I can use.**

And these three laws have been helpful to me in many situations, especially in my language learning.

The mind of man is capable of anything — because everything is in it, all the past as well as all the future.
Joseph Conrad

Postscript

No endings, only cycles …
It's a cold morning, I'm warming my hands and heart around a warm mug. I wait a moment to contemplate the magic of heat and cold. I pour a little cold cream into the hot coffee and watch as it sinks out of sight and then … as it heats up, it comes streaming up to the surface, exploding in subtle hues on the surface in exquisite patterns – *coffee fireworks*! It's a seldom-cherished wonder, but it's there for you if you want it. It's everywhere if you want it!

All the wonder of the world is there inside you, ready to come streaming up and out. Share it with others, tell them about it. Let it be.

APPENDIX 2
Reminders * Think about it, then DO IT!

Have you tried these yet?

1. Have you thought about where you are on your roller coaster? Have you been going up or down recently? What has made you go up or down? What could you do or stop doing to improve your feelings about your language learning?

2. When was the last time you helped a classmate learn something? List things you can do to help your classmates learn. Speak to other non-natives in your target language. Ask them to help you and to explain things to you. When you help other people learn, you help yourself as well.

3. Have you made any good mistakes lately? If not, you may not be risking enough to learn. Dare to try something new!

4. Have you tried shadowing your teachers and conversation partners recently? Sometimes it takes a few tries to do it really effectively, so that you will notice the difference. You can surprise yourself. Write "Shadow" on your hand to remind yourself to do it.

5. What songs have you learned lately?

6. What are the ways that you normally use to try to remember things? What are some other ways that you might try?

7. SMILE! And be serious about doing it often. It's good for you, and can make you happier and more intelligent.

8. How much are you deciding what mood you want to be in and what things mean to you?

9. What time is it now?

10. Have you made a personalized cassette recently of the things YOU want to learn?

11. What is the relationship between juggling and learning a language?

12. What are the ABCs of controlling your emotions?

13. Who *must* you *always blame* for *all* the little things that become *catastrophes*?

14. How much more are you learning by shadowing and summarizing together?

15. How balanced have your Passion, Vision and Action been recently?

16. What are your short-term goals for this week?

17. Compare yourself with yourself a year ago, and a few months ago. How have you improved?

18. What language have you SPURRed lately?

19. What language have you done input and output flooding with?

20. Think of a teacher you would like to help teach you better. What could you tell them?

21. How balanced have your Want To, your Know How To, and your Chance To been recently?

22. How have you changed your environment to help you learn more? What things do you DO to learn more? What new skills are you learning? What are your beliefs about your ability to learn? What kind of identities do you have?

23. Have you told anybody (reformulated) any of my stories recently?

24. Have you taught any of the songs (see Appendix 5) to anyone?

APPENDIX 3
Inventory of Beliefs about Language Learning

Below are beliefs that some people have about learning foreign languages.
Read each statement and then decide if you:

1. strongly agree
2. agree
3. disagree, or
4. strongly disagree.

Put your answer-numbers in the left-hand margin, except for Questions 4 and 13 which are slightly different; for them you should put the letter of the answer you choose in the margin. There are no right or wrong answers.

1. It is easier for children than adults to learn a foreign language.
2. Some people have a special ability for learning foreign languages.
3. Some languages are easier to learn than others.
4. Your target language is:
    (a) a very difficult language
    (b) a difficult language
    (c) a language of medium difficulty
    (d) an easy language
    (e) a very easy language.
5. I believe that I will learn to speak my target language very well.
6. People from my country are good at learning foreign languages.
7. It is important to speak with an excellent pronunciation.
8. It is necessary to know about the target culture in order to speak their language.
9. You shouldn't say anything until you can say it correctly.
10. It is easier for someone who already speaks a foreign language to learn another one.
11. People who are good at mathematics or science are not good at learning foreign languages.
12. It is best to learn in the country where the language is spoken.
13. If someone spent one hour a day learning a language, how long would it take them to speak the language very well?
    (a) less than a year
    (b) 1—2 years
    (c) 3—5 years
    (d) 5—10 years
    (e) You can't learn a language in one hour a day.

14. I enjoy practising speaking with people.
15. If you don't know a word, it's okay to guess.
16. I have a special ability for learning foreign languages.
17. The most important part of learning a foreign language is learning vocabulary words.
18. It is important to repeat and practise a lot.
19. Women are better than men at learning foreign languages.
20. People in my country feel that it is important to speak foreign languages.

21. I feel timid speaking a foreign language with other people.
22. If beginner students are permitted to make errors, it will be difficult for them to speak correctly later on.
23. The most important part of learning a foreign language is learning the grammar.
24. I would like to learn a foreign language so that I can know foreigners better.
25. It is easier to speak than to understand a foreign language.
26. It is important to practise with cassettes or videos.
27. Learning a foreign language is different from learning other academic subjects.
28. The most important part of learning a foreign language is learning how to translate from my native language.
29. If I learn the foreign language very well, I will have better opportunities for a good job.
30. People who speak more than one language are very intelligent.
31. I want to learn to speak the foreign language well.
32. I would like to have foreign friends.
33. Everyone can learn to speak a foreign language.
34. It is easier to read and write in a foreign language than to speak and understand it.
35. I am what I eat.
36. I am what I say.
37. I am what I think.
38. I am what I believe.
39. I am like the people I am most with.
40. I am what people say I am.
41. I am what I pretend to be.
42. I am what has happened to me.

ESL Student Version (adapted by TM)
(1—34 adapted from Horowitz E. K. in
Learner Strategies in Language Learning
Wenden & Rubin (eds.) Prentice Hall
1987 p 127)

APPENDIX 4
Brain Play Summary

A →	B →	C
Something happens	We think something	We feel something

FRIB
Fact   It's raining.
Rational belief   Sometimes it rains and I can't play tennis.
Irrational belief It always rains when I want to play tennis.

Four junkthoughts:

Over generalizing
It always rains when ...
Nobody, everybody, never, only, etc.
To challenge this, ask: Always? Everyone? Never? etc

Catastrophizing
I'll *die* if I fail this test!
It will be just *horrible* if I'm late!
To challenge this, ask: Really? Can I have your lunch if you die?
                            Hey, I think it will also be the end of the world!

Copping out
I was late because I had a phone call at the last minute.
It's the students' fault if they don't learn.
To challenge this, say: You poor thing – other people do cause you problems.
                            You're right – there's absolutely nothing you can do about it.

Demanding
You must write all these letters today!
I have to get an A!
To challenge this, ask: What will happen if you don't?

The four junkthoughts are irrational beliefs. When they occur in position B, then they can cause problems and negative feelings. Recognizing them in ourselves and others helps us to monitor what is going on in our brains – and then we can challenge them if it's okay to do so.

APPENDIX 5
Songs and Jazz Chants

A Song for all Languages! Five Ways to Happiness
Tune, *The 12 Days of Christmas*

English: When You Want to be Happy (Tim Murphey)
When you want to be happy, there's (*) thing(s) you can do…

       (* one, two, three, four, five)

1. Smile from ear to ear.
2. Breathe in deep, and
3. Look up at the sky
4. Sing a melody
5. Dare to show your love

日本語: **幸せになりたい時は**

(Sanae Takenaka, MakikoTakemura, Atsuko Suga)

幸せになりたい時は・・・

1. 思いっきり笑おう
2. 深呼吸して 思いっきり笑おう
3. 空を見て 深呼吸して 思いっきり笑おう
4. 歌を歌って 空を見て 深呼吸して 思いっきり笑おう
5. 愛をしめそう 歌を歌って 空を見て 深呼吸して 思いっきり笑おう

French: Pour être heureux (Christine Vendredi-Auzanneau)
Pour être heureux, il y a (*) chose(s) à faire

      (* une, deux, trois, quatre, cinq)

1. Faites un sourire éclatant.
2. Respirez à fond, et
3. Regardez le ciel
4. Chantez une chanson
5. Osez montrer votre amour

German: Willst du 'gluecklich sein   (Markus Rude)
Willst du 'gluecklich sein, brauchst du eines nur zu tun,
Willst du 'gluecklich sein, kannst du (#) Dinge tun, (# zwei, drei, vier, fuenf)
1. lach von Ohr zu Ohr.
2. atme tief ein, lach von Ohr zu Ohr.
3. schau zum Himmel auf, atme tief ein, lach von Ohr zu Ohr.
4. sing ein Lied, schau zum Himmel auf, atme tief ein, lach von Ohr zu Ohr.
5. zeig dass du liebst, sing ein Lied, schau zum Himmel auf, atme tief ein, lach von Ohr zu Ohr.

Try to memorize this song so that you can sing it without looking at the words. In order to memorize it, sing it to yourself as often as you can. Your memory will remember it better if you **act out** the different parts. When you sing "smile" **SMILE**! Do the things it says, and you will remember it easily after two or three repetitions.

Another way to help you memorize it is to teach it to at least two people. Explain the words and ideas. Get them to sing it with you. Get them happy about the song. You'll know you have done a good job when they ask you for a copy of the words. Have fun!

The Twelve Days of Christmas has always been a favourite of mine. However, I regretted that it didn't contain more useful language for my students. (The message seemed too commercial, too!) So a few years ago I wrote these other words to the melody, for positive use in my English classes (Murphey 1993, 1995), to be sung at any time, not just at Christmas. I even rewrote it in Japanese (with some friendly help) for my own learning (Murphey 1995b). However, the 12 lines really taxed my students (and me), and so in the last few years I have been calling it the 'Five Ways to Happiness' (Learning Strategy No 1: KISS – Keep It Short & Simple), and it has worked wonderfully. More recently, some colleagues and I translated it into French and German. It has also become a tool to show you how you can control your emotional state by changing your body posture.

Some of my students used it for their senior theses, and investigated its use with junior high school students and others. We found this:

· solid research that shows that *smiling* and laughing move facial muscles that send messages to the brain, releasing endorphins (chemicals) in our bodies that kill pain. People who smile actually make themselves feel better, and suffer less pain, because they have a better chemical balance in their bodies.

· lots of research also shows that if you don't *breathe* … you die. Better than that – when you breathe deeply, you get more oxygen into the brain and you think more clearly.

· *Looking up* is where you go to dream, visualize, and create your mission.

· *Singing* does much the same as smiling and breathing, and

· *Daring to show your love* gives you good relationships and helps you develop emotional intelligence.

Research also shows that people who enjoy longevity (a long life) sing a lot and express their emotions.

I tell my students that the posture opposite to the first three lines of the song creates a recipe for depression. To counterbalance this, people can bring themselves out of a depressed state by looking up, breathing deeply, and smiling. (Try it yourself; go ahead – no one is looking – try it!) That same posture of depression is also the posture that's used in test-taking and studying. So tell your students that they will do better in tests if they *pause a few times* and *look up and smile and take a deep breath.* They will also probably drive the teacher crazy with curiosity about what's on the ceiling!

Murphey, T. (1993). 'Twelve Ways to Blissness' *Anchor Point* Dec. pp 18—19,
Murphey, T. (1995a). 'Twelve Ways to Blissness' *Modern English Teacher* 4 (1) pp 42—43

Jazz Chant My Routine

(Keep a beat on the **bold words,** and stress them)

One
When I get **up**
I **make** my **bed**
I **clean** my **room**
and **brush** my **teeth**

I **go** to **breakfast**
Go to **school**
drink some **coffee**
and **read** the **pa**per

After school
I **might** go **jog**ging
I **might** go **sailing**
or **may**be **swim**ming

After dinner
I **might** go **danc**ing
See a **mov**ie
Or **talk** to **friends**

I'll **take** a **show**er
Brush my **teeth**
Go to **bed**
and **have** sweet **dreams**

That's enough
Don't you **think**
And **what** about **you**
What about **you**?

Two

And **then what**?
What next?

And **then what** ?
What next?

And **then** what?
What next?

And **then what**?
What next?

And **then what**?
What next?

Oh **I'm** too **lazy**
Much too **tired**
Thanks the **same**
Thanks the **same**

I Love Misteakes

Doya doya doya doya doya doya doya doya doya doya doya do
Doya doya doya doya doya doya doya doya doya doya doya do
Do you dare to dare to dare to love to love to love
Do you dare to dare to dare to love to love to love

If I make a little Misteake
Well that's just part of mY perfect plan
Being perfectly me
You see, I need my Misteakes
To make me what I want to be

Do you dare to dare to dare to love to love to love your Misteakes
Doya doya doya doya doya doya doya doya doya doya doya do
Doya doya doya doya doya doya doya doya doya doya doya do

(Singing Group Won)
I love Misteakes, I love Mistaykes, I love Misteaks, I love Miss takes

(Singing Group Too)
They show I'm human
They show I'm learning
They show I'm risking
They show I'm living!

Note – doya: "You" is often pronounced "ya" in rapid English speech. Someone who asks you a question may begin with "Doya". For example, "Doya like to play tennis?" Of course, we usually don't write it that way, except in a song or in dialogue in a book.

Tasks
1. Tell a friend or partner in class about a mistake that you recently made. As you tell it, make it funny.
2. Tell three people outside class a funny story about a mistake, and write a short report about their reactions. Tell them either your own story, from no. 1 above, or tell them a friend's story but pretend it was really you who had done it.
3. Get a partner to tell you about a mistake that she or he has recently made. Then tell another partner about it in a funny way, pretending it was you who had made the mistake.

Great misteakes
Columbus thought he was going to India.
X-rays, radioactivity and vaccines were all discovered through mistakes having been made.

Wherdaya howdaya whadaya whodaya
(We all belong in the zoo)
Fast 'n' Natural   **Tim Murphey**

Wherdaya Wherdaya Wherdaya Wherdaya Wherdaya come from, friend?
Howdaya Howdaya Howdaya Howdaya Howdaya like it here?
Whadaya Whadaya Whadaya Whadaya Whadaya wanna drink?
Whodaya Whodaya Whodaya Whodaya Whodaya love so dear?

Wherdaya come from, friend? Howdaya like it here?
Whadaya wanna drink? Whodaya love so dear?
I come from over there, and I really like it here
I'd like another drink and I love you all so dear

Wherdaya howdaya whadaya whodaya, we all belong in the zoo
(Repeat once, faster, and then repeat the last line lots of times – see how fast you can go!)

Fast native pronunciation = simplification
The phrases below on the left are standard written English. But most English speakers run the words together. This happens in all languages to some extent.

1. What have you been up to?	Whadaya	been up to?
2. What are you going to do?	Whadaya	gonna* do?
3. What do you want to do?	Whadaya	wanna do?

* 'going to' gets reduced in, eg, 'I'm gonna go to a film – doya wanna come too?'
   but not in 'I'm **going to** a film – doya wanna come too?'
(The words are reduced when 'going to' means a plan to do something, but they're spoken in full for actual movement.)

This simplification–reduction also explains how the word 'and' becomes 'n', as in cup 'n' saucer. Practise these with a friend:
me 'n' you//boys 'n' girls   // up 'n' down//in 'n' out / / fast 'n' natural

Tasks
1. Think of questions, using these beginnings, that you would like to ask somebody:
   Where do you (Wherdaya)_____?
   How do you (Howdaya)_____?
   What do you (Whadaya)_____?
   What are you (Whadaya) _____?
   Who do you (Whodaya)_____?

2. Now ask your partner these questions using the Fast 'n' Natural.

3. Take down your partner's phone number and call him/her up tonight, asking three questions in the Fast 'n' Natural.

APPENDIX 6
Juggling Manga

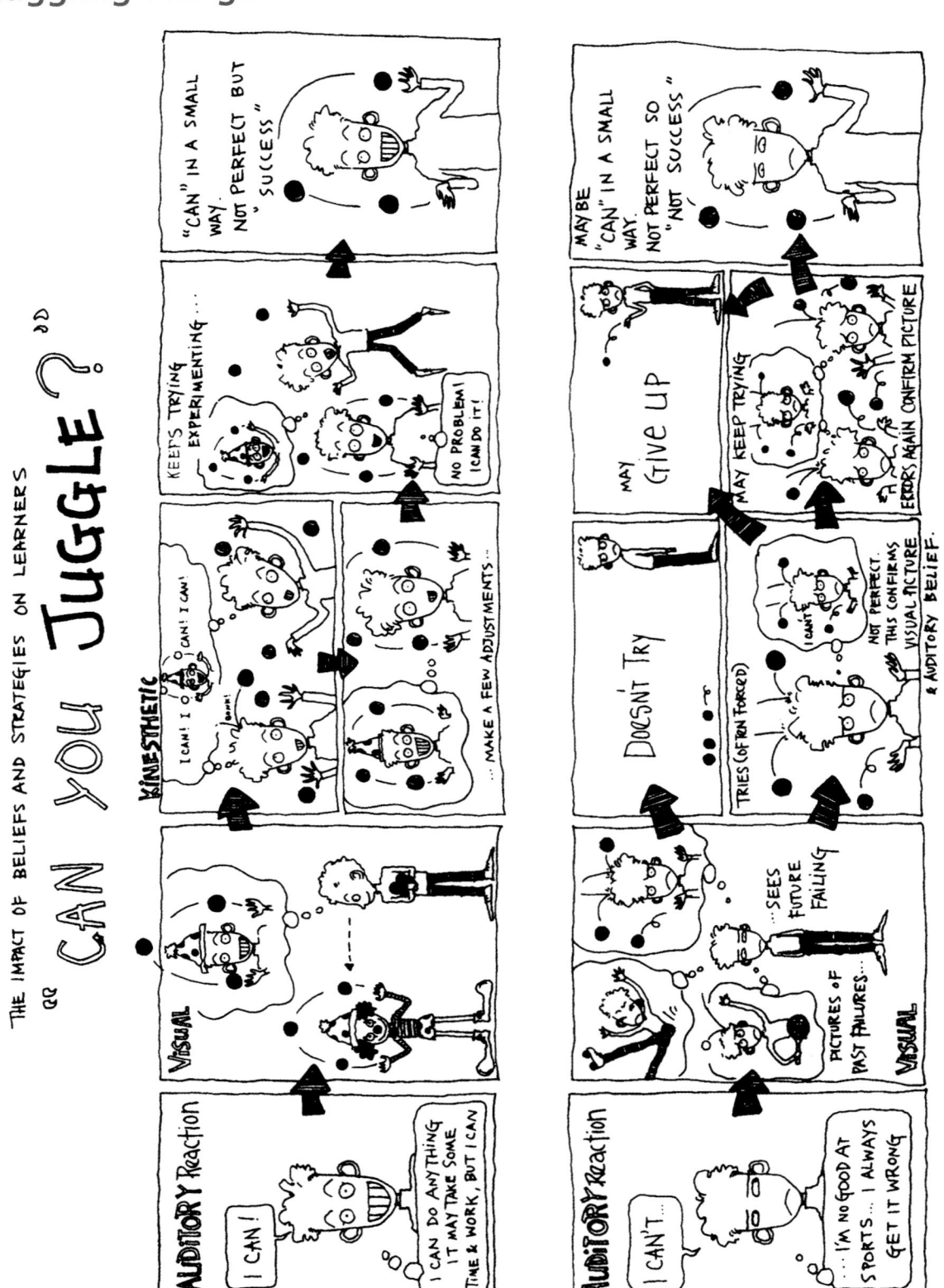